JUSTICE SANDRA DAY O'CONNOR

Studies in American Constitutionalism
General Editors: Gary J. Jacobsohn and Richard E. Morgan

JUSTICE SANDRA DAY O'CONNOR

Strategist on the Supreme Court

Nancy Maveety

ROWMAN & LITTLEFIELD PUBLISHERS, INC.
Lanham • Boulder • New York • London

ROWMAN & LITTLEFIELD PUBLISHERS, INC.

Published in the United States of America
by Rowman & Littlefield Publishers, Inc.
4720 Boston Way, Lanham, Maryland 20706

3 Henrietta Street
London WC2E 8LU, England

British Cataloging in Publication Information Available

Library of Congress Cataloging-in-Publication Data
Maveety, Nancy.
Justice Sandra Day O'Connor : strategist on the Supreme Court /
Nancy Maveety.
p.   cm. — (Studies in American constitutionalism)
Includes bibliographical references and index.
1. O'Connor, Sandra Day 1930—Influence.   2. Judicial Process—
United States.   3. United States.   Supreme Court.   4. Conservatism—
United States.   I. Title.   II. Series.
KF8745.O25M38   1996   347.73'2634—dc20   [347.3073534]   95-52533   CIP

ISBN 0–8476–8194-7 (cloth : alk. paper)
ISBN 0–8476–8195-5 (pbk. : alk. paper)

Printed in the United States of America

♾ ™ The paper used in this publication meets the minimum requirements of
American National Standard for Information Sciences—Permanence of
Paper for Printed Library Materials, ANSI Z39.48–1984.

For Ma

Contents

Preface

It is a risky endeavor to execute a study of the juridical behavior and jurisprudential contributions of a sitting Supreme Court justice. Often, a jurist's import to a judicial era of the High Court is only fully appreciated long after his or her term of service. This is the advantage of revisionist histories. There is a certain utility, however, to contemporary reflection on the current Court and its personnel. Without empirically valid theory about the current Court's decision-making processes, its outputs are difficult to assess. In other words, without plausible explanations as to why and how the justices have come to various decisions, their contributions as policy makers cannot be understood.

Having said this, I should clarify that my aim in this study of sitting Associate Justice Sandra Day O'Connor is to provide a balanced view of a much neglected jurist. My objective is to show that O'Connor has been a more sophisticated and influential judicial actor than initial observations indicated. Because so many early commentaries on O'Connor focused on her status as a "famous first"—the first woman appointed to serve on the Supreme Court—her gender notoriety tended to overshadow her work on the bench. But on closer examination of O'Connor's opinions and coalitional actions, it becomes clear that she has been a key strategist shaping the collective outputs of the Burger and Rehnquist Courts. To avoid overstating this thesis, I should make clear at the outset that I am not claiming for O'Connor some power-behind-the-throne status; such an argument would be empirically unverified and unverifiable. Rather, I am simply suggesting that as we contemporary Court watchers attempt to understand and interpret the work of the current Court, we should not underestimate the role that O'Connor has played in shaping both doctrine and decision-making conventions. Because her contributions to her Court have been both jurisprudential and institutional in nature, she has made a definitive mark on the conservatism of the contemporary Court.

In coming to this understanding of Justice O'Connor, I have been assisted along the way by valuable insights from colleagues (and occasional encouragements which took the form of, "Oh, are you still working on that book?"). The foundation for much of this study lies in my earlier coauthored work with Robert C. Bradley. In many ways, our initial consideration of O'Connor the jurist was a result of his inspiration. Although this study, its merits, and its flaws, are my own responsibility, Bob has been a valued collaborator on the several articles and papers that prefigure this book. He also deserves the credit for securing a written interview with Justice Sandra Day O'Connor, the content of which I rely on for part of the analysis in chapter 2.

Careful study of any subject requires archival work, which itself often requires research support from a benefactor. I have been fortunate to have been able to consult the archives of the Library of Congress—specifically, the collected papers of Associate Justice Thurgood Marshall. I am grateful for the research support provided by Tulane University and the Murphy Institute of Political Economy, which allowed me valuable time and opportunity to consult these papers for my study of the opinion-writing and voting behaviors of Justice O'Connor.

Finally, and as every author knows, final preparation of a manuscript can be a laborious task. I was aided in completing this task by the research assistance efforts of Juan Carlos Gamboa. Without his help, I would surely have taxed the patience of my editor, Jon Sisk, for whose support, encouragement, and endorsement I am greatly indebted. The final manuscript was also greatly improved by the keen and incisive commentary of Mark Graeber and Gary Jacobsohn, and the practical counsel of Steve Wrinn.

I can only hope that readers will find this work as thought provoking as I find its subject.

Chapter One

Introduction: the Accommodationist Judge

> A few years ago, it would have seemed foolhardy to predict
> that O'Connor would be remembered in future textbooks for
> much of anything beyond the quaintness of her gender. But
> because of the shifting alliances of the court as well as her
> own judicial temperament, O'Connor is carving a substantive
> place in history.[1]

Justice Sandra Day O'Connor, appointed to the Supreme Court by
President Ronald Reagan in 1981, has served during one of the most
politicized and polarized periods of the Court's history. During her
tenure the Court has been ideologically divided as well as the center of
various controversies—over the confirmation process, constitutional
interpretation, and the legal resolution of contentious social issues. Yet
O'Connor the judge seems remarkably unaffected by this storm center;
unlike some of her colleagues, whose political orientations and ideological pet peeves are well known, O'Connor has not acquired a reputation for partisan judicial politics.

Justice O'Connor has been a figure of political significance, nevertheless, but for a different reason. O'Connor is, of course, the first
woman appointed to the Supreme Court.[2] Invariably, court commentators assessing her impact on the Court have made reference to her
gender. Certainly, O'Connor's status as the first woman on the Court
is notable, but it is somewhat disappointing that after more than a
decade of juridical service, her status as a "famous first" is still so
central to scholarly discussions of her work.

While her gender was clearly relevant to the political motivations
behind her appointment, it is not necessarily the primary factor influencing her juridical views. Many judicial scholars have persisted,

1

however, in viewing O'Connor and her work through the lens of "women's interests" (e.g., O'Connor and Segal 1990), despite the limited heuristic utility of this approach.[3] Other scholars identify in O'Connor the attributes of a "feminine" decision-making style (Sherry 1986; Behuniak-Long 1992), although this tells us little about the content of her jurisprudence or her impact as a jurist.[4]

The gender-based analysis of O'Connor is disappointing because it has perpetuated scholarly oversight of O'Connor's truly remarkable characteristics as a judicial actor. Simply put, O'Connor has been central to the moderate conservatives' presence on the Court during the later Burger years, as well as their predominance on the current Rehnquist Court. Even more important, O'Connor has inaugurated a post-legal realist, fact-centered jurisprudence that has deideologized the Court's judicial standards and, to some extent, its decision-making. Indeed, O'Connor's avoidance of any firm and broadly applicable judicial standard has functioned as both a jurisprudential and a judicial strategy.[5]

Nevertheless, scholars have generally given scant attention to her role in influencing the collective output of the Burger and Rehnquist Courts—in many cases, failing to see beyond O'Connor's gender. One explanation for this lies in the theoretical foundation of judicial process studies. Many such judicial studies incline toward an attitudinal model of judicial behavior (e.g., Segal and Spaeth 1993), which identifies a behavioral correlation between a judge's votes, attitudinal preferences, and background attributes or characteristics.[6] This approach is particularly predominant in analyses of Supreme Court decision-making processes (Brace and Hall 1993, 916–19). The attitudinal model seeks to explain both individual judicial voting patterns and the presence of ideological blocs of justices. Many judicial process studies thus tend to emphasize the relationship between judicial background variables and judicial support for certain issues, claimants, or ideological positions (Tate 1981). According to this approach, O'Connor's gender stands out as a potentially salient background characteristic. The attitudinal model, however, is somewhat inapt for analyzing the coalitional contributions of a judge like O'Connor, who is frequently characterized as a judge without a judicial ideology. The model assumes that both individual and bloc voting patterns have attitudinal and therefore ideological bases; thus, it could misconstrue O'Connor's predilection for compromise solutions and fact-based resolutions as behaviors inconsistent with ideological consistency and intellectual credibility.

A second explanation for the lack of appreciation of O'Connor's

influence on the Court is related to both her gender and her characterization as a justice without a developed jurisprudence. Arguably, the
initial scholarly fixation on the relevance of her gender established
certain presumptions about O'Connor. Most of these initial studies
addressed O'Connor's position on feminist politics and causes—
presuming that her most distinctive background characteristic was also
the *most* salient to her judicial worldview. Women's issues, in other
words, were assumed to be the key to O'Connor's ideology: she was
either a liberal feminist[7] or some kind of conservative Republican
apologist. O'Connor, of course, is neither an advocate nor a prac-
titioner of feminist jurisprudence,[8] and certain studies have registered
a palpable dismay at this finding; but it seems that once O'Connor was
dismissed as an unsatisfactory feminist, she was also assumed to be a
net loss as a juridical strategist. Her nonideological, pragmatic approach to all legal issues, including those concerning women, was
considered unsophisticated and therefore ineffectual.

It seems equally plausible, however, that a judge, particularly one
with a legislative career history, can be a significant force on a
collegial court without having a concrete ideological agenda—indeed,
O'Connor's brand of pragmatic legal reasoning has consistently affected the Court's collective output in important ways. Her approach
leads more often to conservative judicial decisions than to radical
policy innovation, and it increasingly guides and structures the Court's
conservatism—even as the Court's center has continued to shift to the
right; yet O'Connor's contribution to the Rehnquist Court's generally
pragmatic conservatism is often overshadowed by the words and
actions of her more ideologically driven conservative colleagues. Judicial ideologues capture the attention of the journalistic and academic
punditocracy but not necessarily that of their judicial colleagues.

This study challenges these early verdicts on O'Connor's place on
the Court and seeks to assess systematically O'Connor's contributions
in shaping the development of constitutional law. O'Connor is best
understood in terms of her *accommodationist strategies*, both jurisprudential and behavioral. *Jurisprudential accommodationism* means an
approach to doctrinal analysis and precedental rule following that is
flexible, contextual, and fact specific. It might entail, for example, the
use of balancing approaches to resolve certain constitutional rights
questions. This jurisprudential dimension concerns the aspect of a
judge's record that legal scholars usually address—a judge's opinion-
based reasoning. *Behavioral accommodationism* refers to a strategic
understanding of voting and coalitional behavior that includes swing

voting, separate opinion writing, and conditional cooperation with political allies. The behavioral dimension concerns the more political and quantifiable aspects of judicial action that social scientists study: votes and alliances.

As an accommodationist jurist, O'Connor can be described and her impact analyzed according to three distinguishable but interrelated tendencies. First, her approach to case fact finding and fact-based decision-making is accurately described as contextual conservatism. She is comparatively moderate to restrained when it comes to overturning precedent and is likely to reason by exception when faced with a case not adequately covered by an existing rule. Her approach to case facts should thus be distinguished from that of legal realism, which focuses on the relevance of empirical evidence and sociological data to guide judicial policy making. O'Connor's case-by-case method of adjudication is best labeled *post*-legal realist, because she uses facts not so much as determinants of decisions, but as a means to contextualize and apply the loosely worded standards she articulates in her opinions. Ideologically, then, her conservatism is not categorical and rule bound, but sensitive to the particular elements and history of specific fact situations (see Maveety and Bradley 1993; Gelfand and Werhan 1990). This distinguishes her approach from the more scholastic and doctrinaire conservatism practiced by some of her fellow GOP appointees.

Second, her coalitional predilections include a propensity to join the winning side of 5–4 majorities on the Court. She seems to consider the influence potential of being part of, if not necessary to, minimal winning coalitions on a collegial decision-making body (Bradley and Maveety 1992b). The tactical maneuver of going along with the majority offers the advantage of influence through bargaining, particularly by a judge uncommitted to a bloc *or* a deeply committed judge who appears or is perceived to be unsure (Murphy 1964, 78, 58). O'Connor's appreciation of the importance of majority-side membership no doubt reflects her experiences as a legislative majority leader. In that capacity she certainly learned the value of compromise to achieve results —and that the nature of a compromise can be greatly affected by those who consistently ally with the majority coalition.

Third, as part of a pragmatic centrism, she pursues the alternative leadership tactic of writing concurring opinions to shape the development of legal doctrine. Unless a court is completely dominated by a unified majority of ideological cohorts, fluidity of judicial choice and shifting coalitional alliances tend to exist; therefore, a judge whose arguments appeal to the greatest number of potential coalition partners can wield significant influence. Use of the concurring strategy is a way to extend this appeal without completely sacrificing one's status as a member of the controlling majority (Maveety and Bradley 1993; Maveety 1991a). This is the case whether the concurror joins the opinion of the Court or only its judgment, for it is the separate concurring voice that is significant.[9]

These three tendencies are the unifying themes through which O'Connor's work on the Court are critically examined in the chapters that follow. This study demonstrates the definitive impact O'Connor has had on both constitutional doctrine and the conventions of collegiality of the contemporary Supreme Court.

As a preliminary and foundational matter, chapter 2 provides a biographical and professional background sketch of Sandra Day O'Connor. Her case is both indicative and not indicative of larger trends concerning women in the law; nonetheless, the chapter attempts to place O'Connor—as lawyer, state representative, career Republican, and jurist—within the larger context of women in the legal profession. By drawing on material from her confirmation hearings, early articles she authored, and interview data, the chapter elucidates some of the background characteristics that do seem relevant to O'Connor's judicial behavior.

Chapters 3 and 4 present an overview of O'Connor's juridical record and contributions. Analysis of O'Connor's written opinions confirms that jurisprudential and behavioral accommodationism are attributes that accurately describe her work and role on the Court. Referring to the three tendencies that make up her judicial accommodationism generally, the chapters summarize O'Connor's juridical record of majority, concurring, and dissenting opinions across a range of legal issue areas. The summary analysis examines the distinctiveness, consistency, and feasibility of her interpretive and decisional approach.

Chapters 5 through 7 focus on specific constitutional areas, concentrating on O'Connor's unique contributions to case law and doctrinal development. By reviewing particular O'Connor majority and separate opinions, each of these chapters shows how O'Connor has been pivotal to the current development of the law in that specific issue area by highlighting the distinctive test or doctrinal formulation that O'Connor generated, showing its decisional origin, and tracing its precedental influence and importance. Each chapter shows that, over time, a coalition of moderate conservatives mobilized around her opinions' legal reasoning, thus affecting the Court's adoption of particular doctrines. Chapter 5 examines the law concerning First Amendment establishment of religion and the related problem of its free exercise. In these opinions O'Connor articulates a model of community tolerance that has interesting links to her philosophy on federalism. Chapter 6 looks at reproductive freedom—specifically, abortion rights and state regulatory prerogatives. These opinions most effectively illustrate that it is her accommodationist tactics and jurisprudence that most accurately define her judicial philosophy, and not some commitment to a substantive or ideological value.[10] Chapter 7 concerns O'Connor's jurisprudence of racial communities of interest and its application to the interrelated issues of race-based electoral districting and race-based affirmative action policies. This legal area is the locus of O'Connor's most recent and, as yet, unappreciated juridical contribution. While some commentators have noted O'Connor's contribution to equal protection doctrine with respect to race discrimination (Note 1991; Palmer 1991), few discussions integrate her views on race-based classifications with the matter of defining political communities of interest and articulating their representability.

After documenting O'Connor's appreciable impact on the Court over the last decade, the concluding chapter argues for greater appreciation of the emergence of her quiet style of leadership. Specifically, O'Connor has successfully utilized a new, more choral convention of cooperative decision-making on the Supreme Court. Given that the process of case discussion among the justices becomes more and more abbreviated over time (Rehnquist 1987; Kornhauser and Sager 1993), negotiation over opinions, their precedental basis, and their reasoning must occur through alternate means. Arguably, O'Connor has introduced a more legislative method of forming opinion coalitions—one that relies heavily on a contextual and serial reasoning process. To a much greater degree than her gender, then, O'Connor's background as the current Court's only former legislator influences both her judicial style and her impact on the judicial institution on which she serves.

The assertion of this study is that O'Connor is neither a judge without a jurisprudence nor a negligible force among "the brethren." She is, rather, the Court's accommodationist strategist and the epitome of the conservatism of the contemporary Court. Having said this, I think it important to note that influence in a small group is highly situational. Classic judicial process studies that follow the small group approach stress that influence or leadership has a social as well as a task-oriented element (Murphy 1964; Danelski 1968; Howard 1968). O'Connor's influence consists more of the latter. The task she performs is mediation. O'Connor has had the good fortune—as a politically moderate conservative—to serve on the Court during periods of appreciable ideological polarization and/or fragmentation among the justices. Such divisions expand the possibilities for influence by centrist or "swing" justices, because their votes become decisive in resolving cases. Much was made, for example, of Justice Lewis Powell's determinative role on the Burger Court (Blasi 1983; cf. Kahn 1994, 113–18; 135ff). O'Connor, too, has played this role, but by working from within winning coalitions rather than through an overt swing vote strategy.

Certain aspects of O'Connor's behavior as an accommodationist judge may challenge traditional understandings of the judicial role. Her utilization of a new, more choral convention of collective decision-making, combined with a more contextual process of legal reasoning, imparts a decidedly legislative character to the judicial process. To what extent have her actions affected the Court as a whole, in terms of both opinion output and bargaining conventions? Has O'Connor's accommodationism left an enduring mark on the judicial institution—inaugurating, perhaps, a revitalization of the seriatim opinion method? These are some of the questions this study considers as it addresses O'Connor's influence as strategist on the Supreme Court.

Notes

1. Kohn 1993, 62. As testimony to the accuracy of this comment, one need only consult Lyle Denniston's extensive portrait of Justice O'Connor for the *Baltimore Sun* on the opening of the 1995 term.

2. In 1993 President Bill Clinton nominated Judge Ruth Bader Ginsburg to replace retiring Justice Byron White. Ginsburg's appointment to the Supreme Court was subsequently confirmed by the Senate, and she began her service with the October 1993 term.

3. There are several conceptual problems with such a gender-based analysis of O'Connor. First is the theoretical problem of defining what "women's interests" are. On this question see Sapiro 1983, and Jonasdottir 1988. Second, even if gender-specific interests exist, they are a minority segment of the judicial docket. Focusing on a jurist's perspective on such issues would therefore result in a somewhat incomplete picture of the judicial actor. Finally, because O'Connor is not a self-avowed feminist activist, a "women's interests" lens would likely produce a distortedly dismissive view of her work on the Court and her importance to current jurisprudential debates.

4. The concept is also so amorphous as to include various forms of

balancing in adjudication, as well as orientations toward the community, the group, and the family as opposed to the individual. Is, then, a states' rights jurisprudence—certainly an orientation toward a community—to be considered an attribute of a feminine decision-making style? Not only is the concept of a "feminine" decision-making style unhelpfully broad, it is also reductionist and essentialist in its construction of "male" and "female" archetypes of thinking. O'Connor herself has raised this objection and has resisted the "feminine voice" construal of her work on the Court (O'Connor 1991, 1553). Although a justice's own self-revelatory statements carry little weight for some judicial scholars, O'Connor's repudiation of a gender-based analysis of her own work must be given some credence in this case.

5. The term "strategy" is used here in the sense first and most eloquently discussed by Walter Murphy in his judicial politics classic *Elements of Judicial Strategy*. For Murphy, strategy refers to "the overall plans under which maneuverings [designed to obtain specific advantages in dealing with colleagues] against specific obstacles are coordinated and for which scarce resources are allocated in order to further the accomplishment of the broad policy objective" (Murphy 1964, 9–10).

6. It should be noted, however, that in emphasizing case fact patterns as stimuli for judicial votes, Segal and Spaeth open the door for consideration of case content—including doctrinal attributes and subtexts—as determinative of both attitudes and decisions.

7. "Liberal feminist" is defined as someone supportive of aggressive reforms that guarantee political and economic opportunities to women denied them because of the strictures of socially constructed gender roles. For a comprehensive definition of the liberal feminist perspective, see Tong 1989.

8. As the concept of "feminist jurisprudence" might be defined and employed by Catherine MacKinnon or Robin West, for example. Feminist jurisprudence draws from the experiences of women and from critical perspectives developed outside the legal discipline to offer analyses of the relationship between law, gender, and power. Feminist jurisprudence is frequently critical of the liberal, "male-assimilationist" view of equality for women because of its limited reformative possibilities. Many feminist legal theorists argue that traditional equality doctrine permits differences between men and women to legitimate conditions of dominance of women; instead, these theorists urge the construction of new legal concepts that take account of the different realities of women's experiences without disparaging the value of these experiences. For a discussion of the repercussions of this approach, see the readings collected in Bartlett and Kennedy 1991.

9. In this way the use of concurrence can work in tandem with majority-side alliance, for the former serves as a camouflage tactic for the latter. As Murphy observes,

> one of the tactics of a bloc should be to conceal as far as possible the fact
> of its existence, lest other justices feel it vital to their interests to form a

counterbloc and so perhaps nullify the advantages of the first bloc. Thus it might be more prudent if on some, perhaps many, issues, the bloc members vote against each other *or at least concur in separate opinions.* (Murphy 1964, 80 [emphasis added])

10. Including a commitment to federalism, which some commentators find the key to her work. I do not disagree that federalism is an important value to O'Connor—particularly in light of her state government experience—but it is not the apotheosis of her juridical views. Her federalism opinions are reviewed in chapters 3 and 4.

Chapter Two

Sandra Day O'Connor: A Bioprofile

The new presence of women in the law has prompted many feminist commentators to ask whether women have . . . different styles, aptitudes or liabilities. Ironically, the move to ask again the question whether women are different merely by virtue of being women recalls the old myths we have struggled to put behind us. Undaunted by the historical resonances, however, more and more writers have suggested that women practice law differently than men. One author has even concluded that *my* opinions differ in a *peculiarly feminine* way from those of my colleagues.

> —Sandra Day O'Connor,
> "Madison Lecture: Portia's Progress"

with the exception of Sandra's obvious aesthetic beauty and her very feminine qualities, in the future it will be difficult at best to determine *any gender* by the reading or interpretation of her decisions.

> —Tony West,
> Testimony to the Senate Judiciary
> Committee
> Hearings on the Nomination of Judge
> O'Connor

Most biographical sketches of Sandra Day O'Connor highlight similar episodes from her personal and professional background: her childhood on an isolated cattle ranch in Arizona; her graduation magna cum laude from Stanford Law School, followed by a single job offer as legal secretary for a private firm; her career in Arizona state legislative politics; and her exclusively state court experience prior to her elevation to the High Court in 1981. Generally, the formative nature of these experiences is viewed by O'Connor's biographers through the lens of gender. Clearly, her experiences as a woman in the legal profession as well as her encounters with gender-based disadvantage influenced her identity as a jurist, but as the above quotation from O'Connor indicates, she does not view her own gender-specific experience as imparting a "different voice" to her judicial decision-making (Davis 1993, 134–35; Songer, Davis, and Haire 1994, 436–37).

In assessing her career history as well as the impact of personal background characteristics, a biographer must be mindful of the views of O'Connor the subject. While judges are not known for their extreme candor regarding their behavior and influences on it, their construction of themselves as judicial actors is not irrelevant to a bioprofile. Both her early professional experiences and the politics of her appointment highlight the relevance of O'Connor's gender to her story as a public figure; yet O'Connor adamantly downplays the relevance of her gender to her juridical makeup. More importantly, in doing so O'Connor repudiates a branch of feminist jurisprudence that she brands a dangerous form of biological essentialism (O'Connor 1991). While gender is thus the lens through which O'Connor's background must be viewed initially, O'Connor's own position on this type of biographical treatment is also part of her constitution as a justice.

This chapter first provides a biographic sketch of the personal and public life of Sandra Day O'Connor. The theme here is the way in which gender was both a barrier and a facilitator with regard to O'Connor's professional career. The chapter then recounts important episodes from O'Connor's confirmation hearings before the Senate Judiciary Committee. The goal here is to profile her state legislative experience and her immersion in the coalitional bargaining game of legislative politics. This background variable—which occasioned some rather pointed senatorial questioning about her legislative record on abortion—has distinguished O'Connor from her Supreme Court contemporaries. Her experience as a state legislator and judge also seems to have given her a degree of trust in state government and courts that well exceeds that of her colleagues (Wermiel 1991, 139). Lastly, the chapter summarizes the judicial philosophy that O'Connor reveals in her published articles and in a brief interview granted to the author. The objective is to address the comparative relevance of the gender factor versus that of the state legislative experience factor in assessing O'Connor the judicial actor.

Sandra Day was born on March 26, 1930, on the Arizona-New Mexico border, the first child of a cattle ranching family. She spent her early years on the Lazy B ranch doing the chores expected of a child growing up on a ranch—driving tractors, fixing fences, branding cattle. Sandra learned to be independent at an early age, for, as a childhood friend explained, "we played with dolls, but we knew what to do with screwdrivers and nails too. Living on a ranch made us very self-sufficient" (Shea 1986, 7). When Sandra reached the age of six, she was sent to live with her maternal grandparents in El Paso, where she could receive a formal education in proper schools. She attended the Radford School for Girls, an exclusive private institution in town. She spent the school months away from home but returned to the ranch each summer, where she lived with siblings Ann and Alan, born in 1938 and 1939, respectively.

Sandra excelled in academics, skipping her final grade at Radford, enrolling in honors classes at Austin High School in El Paso, and graduating early at age sixteen. She then attended Stanford University and majored in economics, refusing—unlike many college women of the 1940s—to shy away from "men's subjects." Pursuing the Stanford option that allowed a student to earn both a bachelor's and a law degree in six years, Sandra graduated third in her law school class in 1952 (behind future Chief Justice William Rehnquist, who graduated first in the class). While in law school, she served as an editor of the *Stanford Law Review* and through her work on the journal met her future husband, John Jay O'Connor III. They married on December 20, 1952, six months after her graduation.

In spite of Sandra O'Connor's distinguished law school career, she was unable to find employment at any of the private law firms in Los Angeles or San Francisco—because of her sex. As she recalled later, "I interviewed with law firms . . . but none had ever hired a woman before as a lawyer, and they were not prepared to do so" (Horner 1990, 33). In the end, she was offered only one job: as a legal secretary for the Los Angeles firm of Gibson, Dunn, and Crutcher. Ironically, one of the firm's partners was future Attorney General William French Smith, who was later charged by President Reagan with calling O'Connor to offer her the position as Associate Justice of the Supreme Court. Looking back, O'Connor displayed a sense of humor about the situation, jesting at the 1990 centennial celebration at the firm:

I want to thank Bill Smith. I can remember as if it were yesterday when he telephoned me on June 26, 1981, to ask if I could go to Washington, D.C. to talk about a position there. Knowing his former association with your firm, I immediately guessed he was planning to offer me a secretarial position—but would it be as Secretary of Labor or Secretary of Commerce? (Wermiel 1991, 133)

The difficulties O'Connor encountered with private law firms led her to explore alternative avenues in the public sector. Because the public service area offered the best opportunities to female lawyers, she focused—like many women in the legal profession then and now—on obtaining a government job (Abel 1989). She soon found work as a deputy county attorney in San Mateo County, Arizona. As she remarked later, her first job "influenced the balance of my life because it demonstrated how much I did enjoy public service" (Horner 1990, 33).

On the birth of her first child in 1957, O'Connor wanted to work part time in order to spend time with her baby son. As this plan ruled out major law firms, O'Connor—again following a career path like that of many women in her profession—opened a neighborhood law practice with another young lawyer (Bodine 1983, 1396). Nevertheless, after the birth of her second son in 1960, O'Connor ceased practicing law in order to devote herself full time to raising her children. Because of John O'Connor's job with a prosperous and prestigious Phoenix law firm, Sandra O'Connor was able to enjoy the privileges available to women of her social class, including that of discretionary employment (Cook 1991, 239). With the birth of a third son in 1962, O'Connor maintained her contacts with the legal world through the traditionally female vehicle of community volunteer work. She was president of the Phoenix Junior League and active in a variety of local civic organizations; she also plunged into local political work in the early 1960s, joining the Republican Party and working as precinct organizer to support Arizona Senator Barry Goldwater in his presidential bid in 1964. Her community involvement was as important to her as her partisan activism, for, as she later observed, "I have always wanted to be part of the process of the dynamics of my community, to help it develop and achieve its goals, to try to make it a good place to live" (Horner 1990, 37), but it was her active role in state Republican politics that would facilitate her return to public life.

O'Connor's reentry to her profession began in 1965 with a post as state assistant attorney general. Four years later, she was tapped by the Arizona Republican Party to fill a vacated seat in the state senate. O'Connor was one of only two women state senators in 1969. She was described by a Democratic senatorial colleague as "a conservative in the conventional sense, but beyond that, she's extremely fair" (Horner 1990, 38). As a Republican state senator, O'Connor was a fiscal conservative with liberal tendencies in some areas, such as gender discrimination and the problems of poor families. While she took the conservative Republican approach to such issues as the death penalty, gun control, and school busing, she fought to remove sex-based references from state laws, reform Arizona's community property laws, and liberalize the state's welfare laws (Heck and Arledge 1986, 997). Her reformative impulses also extended to the areas of bilingual education programs, antipollution regulation, and support for the passage of the Equal Rights Amendment (Kohn 1993, 18; Horner 1990, 41). O'Connor proved to be a success in the Senate, winning reelection to her seat in 1970 and 1972 and becoming the first woman nationally to be elected as majority leader in a state senate. Despite this, she has said about her time in the Arizona legislature: "I was never one of the boys" (Kohn 1993, 62).

Perhaps prompted by this dissatisfaction, O'Connor left legislative politics and returned to the law. In 1974 she successfully ran for election as trial judge on the Maricopa County Superior Court, campaigning "as a citizen, a wife, and a mother" on the issue of law and order (Horner 1990, 45). On the small, general jurisdiction trial court, O'Connor acquired the reputation of being a tough judge who prepared thoroughly and expected others to do the same—foreshadowing her approach on the High Bench (Wermiel 1991, 131). In 1979, Democratic Governor Bruce Babbitt elevated O'Connor to fill a new vacancy on the Arizona Court of Appeals, an intermediate state appellate court. At the time some political observers speculated that Babbitt had offered her the judgeship to remove a potentially daunting rival from the electoral arena. While the Arizona Republican Party (and U.S. Senator Barry Goldwater) had urged O'Connor to run for governor against Babbitt in 1978, Babbitt denied any political motivation to his nomination (Horner 1990, 49).

During her eighteen-month tenure on the court of appeals, O'Connor authored twenty-nine published opinions, mostly dealing with routine criminal and commercial matters. In both her trial and appellate judicial capacities, she earned high ratings from the Arizona State Bar Association, which gave her top scores for thoroughness and meticulously written opinions. Evaluations rated her somewhat lower on her personal dealings with attorneys, some of whom bristled at her no-nonsense, crisply businesslike approach (Horner 1990, 51). For O'Connor, efficiency and scrupulous attention to detail came before cordiality and collegiality. This particularistic orientation would continue during her service on the U.S. Supreme Court, yet as a former colleague on the Arizona appeals court remarked in 1981, following Reagan's nomination of O'Connor to the High Court, "she always assumes the leadership role" (Horner 1990, 55).

One commentator has summarized O'Connor's pre-Court experience in this harsh light: "As an overqualified woman who found her opportunities only in minor public offices below the national level, she developed a commitment to state and local government, legislative responsibility, and judicial modesty" (Cook 1991, 239). These latter traits were very much in emphasis during her September 1981 confirmation hearings before the Senate Judiciary Committee and, in fact, have colored her Supreme Court career; but it is important to remember that these traits were, in part, the product of gender-specific professional barriers. O'Connor's experience as a state legislator and trial judge meant that she brought unique style, skills, and knowledge to the job of Supreme Court decision-making, but this experience was the result of the slow-track professional options available to her as a woman in the law. "The gender factor" thus did shape O'Connor's professional career pattern and juridical style—by creating the discriminatory barriers that led to her acquisition of legislative experience and legislative skills.

Court scholars speculate that her views on the limited role of the federal courts can be attributed to her background in state government (Savage 1990, 225; Roberts 1991, 100), a connection O'Connor herself acknowledged (Hearings 1981, at 57). It also seems clear that O'Connor's preference for balancing over categorization in judging (Note 1993, 923–28; Sullivan 1993, 248–50; Sullivan, 1992a) is also a feature of her legislative background. She has been somewhat more opaque as to this linkage—"I do well understand," she stated during her confirmation hearings, "the difference between legislating and judging" (Hearings 1981, at 68); nevertheless, O'Connor more than once characterized her mode of judicial decision-making as approaching each case as a unique set of facts with some law applicable to it (Hearings 1981, at 94, 103). This emphasis on the context of cases— over ideological agendas or even precedents—seemed to mark O'Connor as a "sensible conservative" (Senator Morris Udall's term, Hearings 1981, at 38), who would use a balancing approach both to find as well as to delimit rights (Note 1993, 928).

Obviously, O'Connor's conservative credentials were one major reason for her nomination to the High Court by President Ronald Reagan in 1981. The other major reason for her appointment was, of course, her gender. As a conservative appointment, O'Connor was, ironically, the beneficiary of "a 'plus factor' form of sex-based affirmative action" (Haggard 1990, 70). Her selection served several political objectives for President Reagan. First and foremost, her appointment fulfilled a 1980 election campaign promise to nominate a woman to the Supreme Court. In doing so, Reagan was able to recover some standing with women's rights groups who had earlier been angered by the scant number of appointments of women in his administration (Shea 1986, 1). Democrats were also pleased with the nomination: as well as being a woman, O'Connor was considered a moderate and the best to be expected from a Republican President (Riggs 1983, 1). The only interest that was visibly distressed by the O'Connor nomination was the New Right, particularly the National Right to Life Committee, which saw the nomination as a violation of Reagan's campaign promise to appoint only candidates who respected the sanctity of human life (Shea 1986, 2). Because O'Connor had a questionable reputation as a state legislator on the issue of abortion and was a supporter of the Equal Rights Amendment, she was suspected of being insufficiently pro-family (Cook 1991, 243-44). As a result, O'Connor's future voting behavior on the issue of abortion became the chief focus of her confirmation hearings before the Senate.

In order to ascertain the direction of her voting on the Court, senators were limited to questioning O'Connor regarding her previous official voting behavior. When it came to distinguishing her juridical standpoint on specific constitutional issues, O'Connor was vague and somewhat unforthcoming. As she explained in her opening statement at the hearings:

> I do not believe that as a nominee I can tell you how I might vote on a particular issue which may come before the Court, or *endorse or criticize specific Supreme Court decisions* presenting issues which may well come before the Court again. To do so would mean that I have prejudged the matter or have morally committed myself to a certain position. Such a statement by me as to how I might resolve a particular issue or what I might do in a future Court action might make it necessary for me to disqualify myself on the matter. This would result in my inability to do my sworn duty; namely, to decide cases that come before the Court.[1]

O'Connor stuck by this statement, recalling it whenever senators attempted to ask her opinion on the decision in *Roe v. Wade*. Several committee members, especially those conservatives wishing to uncover information as to O'Connor's philosophy on abortion and privacy rights, were angered by this stipulation. The senators' displeasure at her unwillingness to comment on issues that might come before the Court in the future reached a frustratingly comic height in this exchange between Republican Senator Jeremiah Denton and Chairman Joseph Biden:

> THE CHAIRMAN. Your time is up now but we will give you more time if you want it.
> SENATOR DENTON. Finding out where she stands on other areas where abortion would be permissible than to save the life of the mother is an area of investigation which seems fruitless.
> THE CHAIRMAN. Would another 15 minutes suffice?
> SENATOR DENTON. I do not know whether another month would do, Mr. Chairman. (Hearings 1981, at 248)

The most that committee members were able to learn were brief explanations of her personal feelings on several issues.[2] On the issue of abortion, O'Connor would only say, "[it] is something that is repugnant to me" (Hearings 1981, at 125).

In order to flesh out the implications of her "personal abhorrence" (O'Connor's phrase; used in colloquy with Senator Dennis DeConcini, Hearings 1981, at 98), conservative senators homed in on her voting on the abortion issue while she was an Arizona legislator. The first of her actions to be questioned was her 1970 committee vote in favor of house bill 20, which would have repealed Arizona's felony statutes for abortion. O'Connor answered that the state's laws were entirely too restrictive at the time, not even allowing rape victims to seek abortion procedures. She was then questioned about the 1973 senate bill 1190, which would have provided family planning services, including "surgical procedures," for minors without parental consent. O'Connor, a co-sponsor of the bill, stated that she interpreted the bill as not including abortions and viewed it more as a means of fostering the availability of contraceptive information. The Judiciary Committee next questioned her about her 1974 vote against Arizona house concurrent memorial 2002, which urged the U.S. Congress to pass a constitutional amendment against abortion. O'Connor responded that she felt the initiative had been drafted too hastily after the *Roe v. Wade* decision. Finally, and most revealingly, O'Connor was questioned concerning her vote in 1974 against an abortion limitation amendment to a stadium construction bill. She explained that, as senate majority leader, it was her duty to discourage nongermane riders to bills and so voted against the amendment (O'Connor colloquy with Senator Strom Thurmond, Hearings 1981, at 60–63).

The stadium construction rider was a particularly interesting episode, because it seemed to illustrate O'Connor's preoccupation with the politics of legislative coalition making. In any case, in all of the above instances, O'Connor avoided the constitutional issue of abortion, focusing instead on the problematic details of each case. This tendency to examine questions contextually, evading constitutional ramifications wherever possible, has followed her to the High Bench, where it has become one of her trademarks as a jurist.

The U.S. Senate confirmation hearings on O'Connor's nomination to the Supreme Court provide further insight into the impact of her state politics career history. For instance, her attitude toward precedent was openly pragmatic: "it is not cast in stone but it is very important" (Hearings 1981, at 83); moreover, when questioned aggressively on abortion policy and the status of the *Roe v. Wade* precedent, O'Connor offered this telling observation: "[I hope] that all of us are receptive and responsive to the acquisition of knowledge and to change based upon that knowledge" (Hearings 1981, at 126). Clearly, O'Connor's philosophy as a jurist—her practical attitude toward the evolutionary but incremental nature of legal policy—reflects an awareness that constitutional theory must be responsive to real circumstances. Her conservatism—both in terms of judicial restraint and policy preferences—is undeniable, but it is tempered. One recent commentator termed O'Connor a "preservative conservative," for whom conservative theory works within the system of precedents without attacking it (Note 1993, 923). O'Connor's predilection for compromise is, arguably, the product of both a legislator's exposure to coalitional bargaining and a state judge's experience with accommodating state law to federal expectations.

O'Connor partially confirms these inferences in some of her off-the-bench statements. In commenting on the extent to which her state government experience prepared her for the office of Supreme Court justice, O'Connor said:

The Court benefits from broad and diverse experiences of its members. My own experience in all three branches of state government gave me a background which differed from a majority of my colleagues. It undoubtedly has helped me understand and appreciate the importance and value of the federal system designed by the Framers of the Constitution. (O'Connor 1993, 1)

O'Connor has also made clear that her work as a state appellate judge was, in many ways, commensurable with her work on the Supreme Court. Regarding her method of statutory interpretation for the construction of federal law, she has observed that she "would have used the same approach as a state court judge reviewing a state statute" (O'Connor 1993, 2).

Interestingly, at one point during her confirmation hearings, O'Connor was asked by Chairman Biden what epitaph she would want on her tombstone. "Here lies a good judge," O'Connor responded (Hearings 1981, at 112). Her judicial character would seem to be the policy-making characteristic she most extolls in herself, and it is also the characteristic most directly linked with her state politics past.

In the end, the "good judge" was confirmed in her appointment to the Supreme Court by a unanimous 99–0 Senate vote; yet despite the intensive questioning by the Senate Judiciary Committee, little was known about the content of her judicial philosophy when she took her seat for the October 1981 term. Indeed, after more than a decade of service on the Court, her jurisprudence remains hard to classify.

While O'Connor's off-the-bench statements and writings provide some guidance, she is nevertheless a profoundly untheoretical, pragmatic jurist. O'Connor is not a prolific academic writer like some of her judicial contemporaries. During the course of her confirmation hearings, the senate committee examined her on a single law review article written on judicial federalism (O'Connor 1981). She has, in fact, reserved her most sustained theoretical rigor for discussions of federalism (O'Connor 1984; see also *Michigan v. Long*, 463 U.S. 1032, 1983). Conversely, she has saved her strongest invective for gender-based models of judging (O'Connor 1991).

An early assessment of O'Connor the jurist labeled her position one of "activist restraint" (Note 1985a, 408). This apparent oxymoron contains a kernal of truth: O'Connor's atheoretical, practical, and contextually situated approach to deciding cases is, at once, results oriented, incrementalist, and self-limiting. She came closest to an explicit acknowledgment of her "discretionary balancing approach" to judicial decision-making (Note 1994, 875), in a 1992 lecture at Albany Law School. In addressing a conference on compelling governmental interest analysis in constitutional law, she offered several recommendations as to how judges should define the proper scope of governmental authority versus assertions of individual liberty. "The impulse," she warned, "may be to draw a *bright-line rule*, but such rules may sacrifice one legitimate claim of entitlement for another in the name of simplicity" (O'Connor 1992, 542 [emphasis added]). Rejecting the simplifying impulse, she proposed balancing tests as "a way of overcoming the problems associated with using historical, bright-line approaches to resolve constitutional ambiguity" (O'Connor 1992, 543). She then went on to recognize that balancing is not without its problems—a chief one being that legal debates too often become entangled with discussion about the mechanics of tests that "complicates issues, obscures common ground, and postpones the achievement of goals" (O'Connor 1992, 544). Interestingly, her solution to the problems inherent in the discretionary balancing of governmental and individual interests was a holistic reference to federalism concerns (O'Connor 1992, 545–46).

This reference to federalism as a practical and normative guidepost seems a further indication of O'Connor's context-specific, results-oriented incrementalism. Some would argue that if there is any unifying theme to O'Connor's opinions, it would appear to be her own brand of federalism; however, it seems equally apparent that she is "quite willing to cast federalism aside with nary a mention when there are paramount principles at stake."[3] Indeed, her very jurisprudence of federalism is one of nontheoretical, activist restraint. For example, she conceives of judicial federalism as a pragmatic and situational balance between state court autonomy and uniformity of federal law. This balance draws its substance from a series of interrelated precedents, developed through the 1980s, that provide doctrinal guidance in particular legal situations (O'Connor 1989, 10–11). Interestingly, O'Connor conceptualizes the judicial federalism relationship with a marital metaphor of cooperation and reciprocal self-restraint[4]: "the marriage between our state and federal courts, like any other marriage, requires each partner to respect the other, to make a special effort to get along together, and to recognize the proper sphere of the other partner" (O'Connor 1989, 12).

Metaphors of gender relations also animate a lecture O'Connor delivered at New York University Law School in 1991, in which she reviewed the history of sex-based distinctions in American law and their dismantling through equal protection litigation.[5] While not particularly theoretical, the address did reveal O'Connor's impatience with what she termed "new feminism's" revival of "the Victorian myth of the 'True Woman' " (O'Connor 1991, 1553). Though acknowledging that furthering gender equality at times requires accommodating differences, such as those concerning reproduction and pregnancy, O'Connor rejected the idea that gender differences deterministically constitute gender-based voices, capacities, and virtues that "establish new categories of 'women's work' to which women are confined and from which men are excluded" (O'Connor 1991, 1557).

Her ideal is clearly that of sex neutrality in political roles; indeed, her own voting behavior on the Court confirms that she does not appear to speak in a voice different from those of her male conservative colleagues (Davis 1993, 138). Nevertheless, she seems sensitive to the fact that this is an ideal that is ahead of its time in American culture (O'Connor 1985). One early commentator summarized "the O'Connor dilemma" in this way: "while she accepts the inevitability of her representative role with grace, she looks ahead to the time when sex identity will lose its significance in the selection of public officials" (Cook 1982, 326); or, one might add, in explanations of those public officials' behavior. Feminism, as a theoretical or political organizing principle, is not a part of O'Connor's jurisprudence.

In the last analysis, O'Connor does not prove to be theoretically motivated by either background variable highlighted at the beginning of the chapter. Neither the gender factor nor the state legislative experience factor generates in O'Connor a theoretically embellished juridical framework of feminism or federalism. O'Connor acknowledges that her experience as a woman in the legal profession and her experiences as a state legislator and judge have helped her to appreciate the complexity and tremendous significance of the issues brought before the Supreme Court (O'Connor 1992, 539; O'Connor 1993, 1; O'Connor 1985, 9–10), but none of these experiences has crystallized into a theory-driven jurisprudential philosophy; thus, with respect to her juridical makeup, the comparative relevance of her gender versus her state politics career is difficult to assess. Perhaps the very balancing that O'Connor espouses as a judge is a feature of her determination not to be impelled by any single factor—whether in the courtroom or in her life.

Notes

1. Statement of Sandra Day O'Connor, Hearings 1981, at 57–58 (emphasis added).

2. In an exchange with Senator Robert Dole, however, O'Connor gave some indication of the content of her views on public funding for abortion. When asked directly whether her sponsorship of Arizona senate bill 1165 (providing Medicaid benefits for only those abortions necessary to save a mother's life)

accurately represented her view on abortion, O'Connor answered, "yes—in general substance" Hearings 1981, at 95.

3. Wermiel 1991, 139. See her opinions in *City of Richmond v. Croson*, 488 U.S. 469, 1989, and *Pacific Mutual Life Insurance Co. v. Haslip*, 111 S.Ct. 1032, 1991 (O'Connor, J., dissenting). Indeed, with regard to the *Croson* decision, dissenting Justice Marshall "could not resist pointing out . . . the impact the decision would have on the interests of federalism" (Wermiel 1991, 140). He commented that "the majority's pronouncements [on minority business set-asides] will invariably discourage or prevent governmental entities, particularly States and localities, from acting to rectify the scourge of past discrimination." 488 U.S. at 529. O'Connor's federalism opinions are discussed in the review of her juridical record in chapters 3 and 4.

4. One might term O'Connor's a-theory of federalism, pace Justice Potter Stewart, an "I know it when I see it" approach.

5. O'Connor has lectured on this topic several times. See the reprinted addresses, "Achievements of Women in the Legal Profession," 1985, and "Women and the Constitution: A Bicentennial Perspective," 1990.

Chapter Three

The Juridical Record: Jurisprudential Accommodationism

If the confirmation experience of Justice Ruth Bader Ginsburg is any indication, women nominees to the Supreme Court have lost their novelty status. One implication of this is that their feminist credentials—or lack thereof—are not presumed to summarize their jurisprudential philosophy. This development was patently obvious during the Senate Judiciary Committee's questioning of Judge Ginsburg. Her professional record of advocacy for women's rights coexisted with an expressed dissatisfaction with the legal justification for abortion rights given in *Roe v. Wade*; yet, despite a surfeit of evidence as to her particular feminist stance, the Senators' questions suggested a realization that a woman's influence on the Court amounted to much more. By contrast, O'Connor's confirmation record and early reception as an appointee marked a less sophisticated way of assessing women on the bench. From the time of her nomination through her early years of service, O'Connor was celebrated, castigated, then grudgingly accepted for her "feminist" position. Only since she has shown that there is more to her juridical mind than the feminist-antifeminist dimension has she been acclaimed for more than her sex.

As both her juridical record and the previous chapter's profile make clear, O'Connor's status as a "famous first" is salient but not necessarily of overarching significance to her judicial career. Certainly, one way to interpret her accommodationist tendencies on the bench is through a Gilliganesque, "feminine voice" model (Sherry 1986; Behuniak-Long 1992); yet such an approach conceals as much as it purportedly reveals about the nature of O'Connor's judicial accommodationism, because it fails to focus on the correct jurisprudential and behavioral factors and to identify them specifically as jurisprudential or behavioral and not gender-related factors.

Moreover, in light of the discussion in the previous chapter, it is also important to clarify that federalism—while an important value for former state judge and state legislator Sandra Day O'Connor—is not the principal explanatory factor of her juridical record. The previous chapter compared the relative importance of two of her key background characteristics—gender and state political service. While both were found to have influenced O'Connor's views of certain policy questions, neither seemed to be of overarching significance for her jurisprudence. As this and the following chapter show, O'Connor's anti-bright-line doctrinal philosophy and commitment to behavioral accommodation are better indicators of her judicial performance than any substantive or ideological position on the rights of states.

Remaining mindful of O'Connor's career history as an experienced legislative bargainer, this assessment of her juridical record begins by focusing on her coalitional behavior in the opinion production process. This refers not to simple bloc voting patterns, but to her approach to the possibilities for strategic action on the bench. Strategic judicial action can be defined as behavior geared toward influencing the collegial decision-making process and the collective production of legal policy. Clearly, collective action problems affect all cooperative decision-making bodies, legislatures as well as multimember courts (Grofman 1982; Spiller 1992; Cameron 1993). For courts, a particular collective action problem pertains to ideology. To what degree will ideological commonalities bind a judicial coalition to a collective opinion that requires two dimensions of agreement: one on the result or policy outcome and the other on the doctrinal reasoning (Maveety 1991)? The bidimensionality of opinion coalitions makes them susceptible to manipulation along these two dimensions of choice (Riker 1986, 144–51). The potential for coalition disruption thus exists through vote trading as well as legal argumentation; these options constitute the avenues for strategic action on the bench.[1]

The centrality of ideology in explaining judicial interagreement and coalitional action is a feature of the dominance of the attitudinal model among judicial process scholars (Schubert 1967). In its most recent and most extensive exposition by Jeffrey Segal and Harold Spaeth, the attitudinal model is described as "hold[ing] that the Supreme Court decides disputes in light of the facts of the case vis-a-vis the ideological attitudes and values of the justices" (Segal and Spaeth 1993, 65);

thus, the conjunction of fact stimulus with attitudinal predisposition produces the judicial vote.

Other judicial process scholars, however, notably those adhering to the "small group" approach, have long postulated the existence of "judicial fluidity." Small group studies argue that judges can be swayed by influences from their colleagues; these studies emphasize that Supreme Court decision-making is a complex phenomenon (Goldman and Jahnige 1985; Brenner 1989; Murphy 1964 and 1966). Judicial fluidity, then, presumes that nonideological, group-dynamic factors affect judicial choice, making it mutable. As stated by fluidity's most eloquent exponent, J. Woodford Howard, "judges change their votes and permit their opinions to be conduits for the ideas of others," for "judging is situational, like most American decision-making, and is apt to be more complex than the simple mirroring of . . . personal belief systems" (Howard 1968). Howard based much of his inference on the conference notes and docket books of Justice Frank Murphy, yet contemporary evidence—the record of conference memoranda and draft opinion circulations found among the Thurgood Marshall Papers at the Library of Congress—also suggests the existence of fluidity in judicial choice on the Supreme Court. This fluidity is key to understanding collegial judicial decision-making; without the possibility of fluidity, strategic judicial action—or, strategic opinion initiation and support—is impossible to contemplate.[2] As Howard concludes regarding the use of ideology as an explanatory variable for judicial votes,

> the intervening variables of *strategy and style* are so critical in judicial decision-making that they cannot be excluded from any stimulus-response model without distorting results and reducing the reliability of the most carefully constructed attitudinal inferences. (Howard 1968)

Judicial ideology is obviously related to judicial coalitional behavior, but in a complex and nontrivial way: ideology constructs the proto-coalitional setting in which interjudicial influence can take place. A Court's ideological profile is thus a useful way to begin assessing its members and their collective policy making. This point is especially clear with respect to Justice O'Connor.

Because O'Connor was appointed by a conservative Republican president and was joining a nominally conservative Court dominated by Nixon appointees, it was assumed that she would provide the ideological glue that would cement a conservative judicial coalition (Witt 1986; Cook 1991). It is true that O'Connor initially aligned herself with the conservative bloc on the Court in keeping with her anticipated conservative position. O'Connor's overall voting behavior in her first three terms on the Court showed an approximate 80-percent agreement rate with her brethren in the conservative bloc (Scheb and Ailshie 1985, 11–12). O'Connor thus became a fourth consistent conservative vote during her early years on the Burger Court, but, arguably, it was this position of being critical to a fledgling coalition—and not conservative ideology per se—that animated O'Connor the judicial actor.

Generally speaking, during O'Connor's tenure ideological similarities have been insufficient to facilitate durable judicial interagreement on the Supreme Court. The ideological polarization of the Burger Court that O'Connor joined is well known; in fact, the failure of Nixon's strict constructionists to dismantle the Warren Court record prompted one contemporaneous study to label the Burger era "the counter-revolution that wasn't" (Blasi 1983; see also Schwartz 1987; Kahn 1994), and, although "conservatives" constitute a voting majority on the current Rehnquist Court, there is no commonly agreed-on philosophy among them. One observer characterized the 1988 term, which had five consistent conservative votes with the arrival of Anthony Kennedy and including O'Connor, as a struggle to put together pluralities or bare majorities (Chemerinsky 1989, 48). For various controversial issues, such as abortion, affirmative action, incendiary speech acts, and church-state relations, differences in judicial philosophy continue to threaten the cohesiveness of the conservative "bloc." Even a shared conservative predisposition among a majority of justices does not mitigate fundamental differences in interpretive philosophies or conceptions of the judicial role.[3]

Simply put, O'Connor's general conservative voting record does not fully express her judicial ideology or her capacity to exercise Court leadership. Her coalitional behavior has not accorded exactly with the expectations of an attitudinal model of judicial behavior. Several studies document the decisive fifth vote that O'Connor has cast on both the Burger and Rehnquist Courts in certain legal areas—most notably, abortion rights and establishment of religion (O'Connor and Segal 1990; Note 1989; Note 1987). In other words, O'Connor has been more of a swing vote, alternating her coalitional alliances, than she has been a predictable ideologue; moreover, this pattern persists across several issue areas and is not limited to a singular sample of cases.

O'Connor has also not adopted a formulaic or categorical jurisprudential philosophy (Kahn 1994, 135; Gelfand and Werhan 1990; Sherry

1986; Feder 1988; Taylor 1989). This may have reflected an awareness of the futility of ideological posturing on a jurisprudentially splintered Court. O'Connor avoided the pitfall of ideological disputation over applicable legal standards, while still frequently joining with the majority side. O'Connor typically announces her doctrinal contributions in separate opinions and as alternatives to a particular majority's ideologically driven and rigidly formulated legal principles. In this way, she has accentuated her influence as a majority coalition member, while maintaining her independence from any one wing of the Court. Her behavior suggests that she capitalized on the fact that, during the Burger and early Rehnquist Court years, no consensus existed on an applicable interpretive philosophy and that the Chief Justice was not an intellectual leader.

In situations where ideology cannot facilitate judicial agreement, an important logistic question arises: how do decisional standards get adopted for use by collegial courts, and where are such standards found? O'Connor's coalitional behavior and decisional strategy may suggest an answer.

During much of her tenure on the Supreme Court, O'Connor has employed a decisional strategy of pragmatic centrism. This includes a predilection for contextual legal reasoning, a case-by-case approach to the formulation of doctrinal principles, and an avoidance of ideological solutions to resolve cases. Her judicial ideology of fact-based reductionism of legal problems has allowed her to align frequently with court majorities while maintaining a capacity for juridical independence.[4] O'Connor's antiformulaic approach to constitutional problems, combined with her generally conservative, incrementalist tendencies, often place her at the fulcrum of intracourt divisions. On the conservative-controlled but jurisprudentially muddled Rehnquist Court, O'Connor's pragmatic centrism thus has allowed her to exert influence over the generation and adoption of decisional standards.

O'Connor's pragmatic centrism takes the form of judicial accommodationism which has both jurisprudential and behavioral dimensions. The jurisprudential accommodationism is shown in the contextual orientation of the standards, or tests, that O'Connor employs to decide certain cases. Jurisprudential accommodationism is also seen in these tests' lack of reliance on or origination in strictly ideological principles. Arguably, O'Connor's accommodationism is based on a proclivity for balancing competing interests within given fact situations, regardless of whether the interests to be balanced are the opposing parties to the case or the contending justices of the Court (VanGeel 1991); thus, her avoidance of the divisive, ideologically derived rules used by some of her conservative colleagues is a function of both jurisprudential and behavioral accommodationism. O'Connor refrains from polarizing solutions, either doctrinally or coalitionally. While giving voice to her own independent sentiments, she still tends to align herself in voting (though not necessarily in decision) with the majority conservative bloc. She manages this by filing concurring opinions—the ultimate expression of agreeing while disagreeing. Her behavioral accommodationism thus involves both a propensity to be part of the winning side and the use of concurrence as an alternative tactic of doctrinal leadership.

The juridical record of O'Connor's opinions clearly shows that jurisprudential and behavioral accommodationism are decisional tendencies unifying her work. Reference to her three interrelated, but distinct and empirically verifiable behaviors— (1) employment of a judicial ideology of fact-based, contextual conservatism, (2) the propensity for joining the winning coalition, and (3) pursuit of the alternative leadership strategy of concurrence—provides a means of categorically summarizing her juridical contributions in majority, concurring, and dissenting opinions on the Supreme Court.

The remainder of this chapter focuses on the content of O'Connor's jurisprudential accommodationism; the subsequent chapter identifies and analyzes the two coalitional tendencies that make up her behavioral accommodationism. The analyses in both chapters draw on the newly available manuscript collection of Associate Justice Thurgood Marshall, whose judicial papers provide insights into the Court's internal workings from 1981 to 1990, which corresponds to O'Connor's first nine years of service on the bench.

In assessing O'Connor's influence on her colleagues and on the production of legal doctrine, these chapters evaluate the consistency and saliency of her distinctive approach to collegial judging. The analysis shows that O'Connor's accommodationist strategies should be construed as integral to the recent Court's derivation and adoption of many of its decisional standards.

Fact-Based Reductionism and Contextual Conservatism

Characterizing O'Connor's judicial ideology as contextual, reductionist conservatism is to say that it is fact driven, not rule driven. In other words, as a judicial policy maker, O'Connor leans toward conservative outcomes but does not derive the reasons or justifications for those outcomes from conservative ideological principles. In a recent piece for the *Harvard Law Review*, Kathleen Sullivan spoke of the division on the contemporary Court between "justices of rules" and "justices of standards" (Sullivan 1992b, 26–27). While the former engage in adjudication by categorization, the latter engage in adjudication by balancing conflicting values. If Scalia typifies the former type of jurist (Brisbin 1989; Brisbin 1990), then O'Connor typifies the latter—so much so, that she is often accused of ad hoc, unprincipled decision-making (Karlan 1993; Grofman 1995). O'Connor's decisions are un-principled in the sense that they reduce legal controversies to key facts, facts that trigger some revised accommodation of existing juris-prudential standards. Her judicial philosophy can thus be labeled reductionist and contextual, because for O'Connor adjudication is a distillatory activity, and its conclusions are always situational, never ecumenical.

Her reductionist, contextual conservatism has two other qualities: an anti-bright-line jurisprudence and an agenda of balancing or accom-modating divergent interests. O'Connor's decisions frequently justify exceptions within rules, arrive at context-specific solutions, or articu-late balancing tests for certain fact situations—all anti-bright-line ana-lytic methods. Because, moreover, O'Connor's doctrinal policies are nonformulaic, they encourage only modest, incremental change and thus have broad appeal to the various moderates and moderate conser-vatives on the Court and can serve as the agents of compromise in contentious legal areas. For O'Connor, jurisprudential flexibilty is both a philosophy of judging and a strategy for collective bargaining.

These decisional tendencies are clearly demonstrated in O'Connor's opinions across a broad range of highly salient issues. For example, in her initial approach to the polarizing abortion question, O'Connor deliberately offered a jurisprudential middle ground. The 1973 ruling in *Roe v. Wade* had established the (in)famous "trimester approach," which balanced a woman's right to terminate a pregnancy with a state's interests in protecting maternal health and fetal life. The *Roe* framework guaranteed the right to abortion in the first trimester but also authorized an ascending scale of permissible state regulation in subsequent trimesters, based on the then-current medical technology regarding obstetric medicine and fetal viability. Over time, the *Roe* approach has become increasingly complicated and controversial, be-cause of advances in obstetric medicine as well as moral objections to abortion on demand. Abortion became an increasingly polarizing issue for the justices, for whom no jurisprudential accommodation seemed to exist.

The O'Connor alternative, first announced in dissent in the 1983 decision of *Akron v. Akron Center for Reproductive Health*, stipulated that a state regulation would have to *"unduly burden"* a woman in her right to choose abortion before heightened scrutiny would be employed by the reviewing court (462 U.S. 416, 461). Justice William Brennan's conference notes on the *Akron* case show that O'Connor's position shifted somewhat from her vote at conference (Marshall Papers, box 315, folder 1). Significantly, the first draft of her dissent complained that technological medical advances had meant that states "may no longer rely on a *'bright line'* that separates permissible from impermissible regulation" of abortion (Marshall Papers, box 314, folder 12, p. 4 [emphasis added]). Consequently, her dissent counseled jettisoning the *Roe* trimester framework because it was "on a collision course with itself." Although the language may not have been uniquely hers,[5] O'Connor's "unduly burdens" test was clearly an effort to replace a bright-line, rule-driven approach with an anti-bright-line, contextual standard. Interestingly, she later claimed that the unduly-burdensome approach had been "embedded" in abortion precedents and had simply been misapplied in *Akron*.[6] This claim suggests the reductionist method of O'Connor the jurist, reading jurisprudential standards out of the fact situations, not the words, of prior rulings.[7]

The "unduly burdens" approach required that state regulation of medical procedures and their accessibility may not impose exaggerated or excessive restraints on a woman's abortion decision. In commenting on the test, one law review article speculated that

> O'Connor may be the "great compromiser" of today's Court and, as such, her standard of review for abortion probably will be adopted by the Court as it struggles to find the proper balance in this tension-filled area. (Note 1989, 342)

This prediction has been partially realized in the Court's more recent abortion rulings. In the 1989 case of *Webster v. Reproductive Health Services*, O'Connor's concurring opinion preserved the *Roe* precedent but applied the "unduly burdens" test to uphold Missouri's restrictions on abortions, including viability testing during the first trimester. As is now known, since the availability of the Thurgood Marshall Papers, her concurring vote in *Webster* was especially pivotal. She defected from Chief Justice Rehnquist's opinion for the Court, forging a consensus at the center that transformed Rehnquist's opinion into a judgment of the Court and Justice Harry Blackmun's dissent into a partial concurrence. While her formulation was not adopted by a majority,[8] Blackmun's opinion alluded favorably to her "unduly burdens" test (492 U.S. 490, 545, n. 6; Note, 1989), and conference memos indicate that the force of her reasoning had persuaded Justice John Paul Stevens to her side (memo of 22 June 1989, Marshall Papers, box 480, folder 6).

O'Connor's coup de grace finally came in 1992 in *Planned Parenthood v. Casey* (112 S.Ct. 2791, 1992). In an unusually collegial effort, the plurality of O'Connor, Kennedy, and David Souter authored a jointly written opinion for the Court, preserving a limited notion of reproductive freedom. In terms of O'Connor's jurisprudential accommodationism, the anti-bright-line language of her joint opinion (112 S.Ct. at 2820–25) attracted a like-minded ally in Justice Souter. *Casey* was itself a cautious, conservative ruling, respecting prior precedent but upholding all save the spousal-notification restrictions on abortion in Pennsylvania, yet this outcome was derived not from a categorical rule, but from a flexible, context-sensitive standard—O'Connor's "unduly burdens" test (112 S.Ct. at 2820–21); indeed, a contemporary commentary on the case praised the *Casey* opinion for enshrining a "regime of toleration" in constitutional law with respect to abortion (Strauss 1992, 28). Clearly, O'Connor's balancing-of-interests approach to reproductive rights was an attempt to circumvent the divisive polarity of her colleagues' ideologically driven tests. In the juridical realm (though perhaps not the political realm), her effort has thus far been successful.

A second area of success for O'Connor's jurisprudential accommodationism was church-state relations. As in the reproductive rights area, O'Connor labored to replace a rule-driven approach with a context-sensitive, anti-bright-line standard for adjudicating church-state entanglements. When O'Connor joined the Court in 1981, it was struggling to apply the "*Lemon* test" to problems of church-state separation. Ironically, the *Lemon* test was ostensibly a balancing approach, not a categorical set of rules,[9] but in the years since its formulation in 1971 the tripartite test had been applied rigidly as well as flexibly, producing inconsistent and seemingly unprincipled results (Kahn 1994, 128). As a doctrine dictating policy outcomes, it satisfied neither "high-wall" separationists nor "low-wall" nonpreferentials.

O'Connor's first intervention in this muddled jurisprudential area was to offer an accommodationist alternative. As with her "unduly

burdens" test, her "endorsement of religion" standard for establishment clause violations was not immediately attractive to the brethren.
Consequently, she initially pursued her alternative through the vehicle
of separate opinions. In the 1984 crèche display case of *Lynch v.
Donnelly* (465 U.S. 668, 1984), O'Connor sided with the five-justice
majority holding that the display did not violate the establishment
clause. She argued in concurrence, however, that her vote turned on
whether the government-sponsored use of a religious symbol conveyed
a message of endorsement of religion, taking into account the context
in which the symbol appears (465 U.S. 668, at 687, 692). Because the
nativity scene was accompanied by secular holiday symbols such as a
Santa's sleigh, candy canes, and Christmas carolers, O'Connor felt
that the crèche's religious message was effectively neutralized. The
context-sensitive and fact-driven nature of her approach is self-
evident; less apparent is the conservatism of her position: she techni-
cally adhered to the *Lemon* precedent by distilling the endorsement
standard from the *Lemon* line of cases.

The *Lynch* case illustrates O'Connor's jurisprudential accommodationism in other ways as well. As the record of conference memos
indicates, the *Lynch* court was already in dispute as to what context
was at issue in the case: the display's physical, spatial setting or its
cultural, seasonal one (Marshall Papers, box 343, folder 5). Chief
Justice Warren Burger, speaking for the majority, felt that the latter
alone adequately secularized the nativity display. Interestingly, in her
fifth and final draft opinion, O'Connor split the difference between
Burger and the dissenters by inserting the word "physical" into a
phrase about "the display of the creche in this particular . . . setting,"
then likening its usage to other permissible cultural acknowledgments
of religion (Marshall Papers, box 343, folder 4). In mediating between
the two views of the relevant context, O'Connor was purposefully
seeking a doctrinal compromise. In doing so as an independent,
concurring voice, O'Connor avoided threatening the majority coalition
but signaled her conditional acceptance of the minority's argument.

O'Connor continued this strategy for forging a compromise position
in subsequent establishment cases. In a 1985 case involving a moment-
of-silence statute, she further clarified that her approach provided
needed analytic content to the *Lemon*-based inquiry into whether a
government's purpose is to *endorse* religion (*Wallace v. Jaffree*, 472
U.S. 38, 67–83, 1985). This time, O'Connor concurred in judgment
with a majority that found an establishment violation. The impact of
O'Connor's endorsement language was apparent during the process of

opinion drafting and circulation: the first draft of Stevens's opinion for the Court directly referenced O'Connor's endorsement principle (Marshall Papers, draft of 29 January 1985, box 362, folder 2); Rehnquist purposively removed from his dissent a phrase about the establishment clause not prohibiting generalized endorsement of prayer (Marshall Papers, fifth draft of 15 May 1985, box 362, folder 1); and successive drafts of Burger's dissent devoted more space to responding to O'Connor's opinion than to the Court's (Marshall Papers, box 362, folder 1).

While a majority has yet to formally embrace the endorsement test as the definitive doctrine for establishment clause questions, it is frequently central to the court's discussion of church-state controversies and pivotal to their resolution. This was clear in the 1989 case of *County of Allegheny v. ACLU* (492 U.S. 573, 1989). *Allegheny* involved two different and separate religious displays: a solitary nativity scene and a menorah accompanied by nonreligious holiday decorations. The record of conference memos reveals that O'Connor was originally among four justices objecting to both displays on establishment grounds; in fact, she was writing the opinion for the dissenters (Marshall Papers, box 477, folder 3). Blackmun's draft opinion for the Court relied heavily and explicitly on O'Connor's reasoning from *Lynch*, arguing that the erosion of establishment clause values is "not susceptible to a single verbal formulation" (draft of 30 May 1989, Marshall Papers, box 477, folder 3, p. 14) and applying the endorsement test to assess the "particular physical setting" in which the menorah occurred (draft of 30 May 1989, Marshall Papers, box 477, folder 3, pp. 17–18; 26). This reaching out to O'Connor was not in vain, as her 6 June 1989 memo to Blackmun indicates: "After reading your thoroughly documented opinion in this difficult case, I have decided to join parts of it and concur in the judgement . . ." (Marshall Papers, box 477, folder 3). As she simultaneously indicated in a memo to Justice William Brennan, this was a change from her conference vote (memo of 6 June 1989, Marshall Papers, box 477, folder 3). While the Blackmun opinion gained only a plurality, his reliance on O'Connor's endorsement approach secured at least the partial alliance of O'Connor and Stevens.

Similarly, in the Court's more recent church-state cases, O'Connor's endorsement test was central to the jurisprudential discussions, though not the definitive basis of any particular ruling; but another justice, Souter, enthusiastically embraced the endorsement of religion approach, arguing that it had "become the foundation of establishment clause jurisprudence" (*Lee v. Weisman*, 112 S.Ct. 2649, 2676, 1992). The acceptance of O'Connor's contextual, fact-driven approach to church-state separation by a working plurality of the Court (O'Connor, Stevens, Blackmun, and Souter) suggests that its formal adoption by the Court is imminent. As a detailed discussion of opinion-writing processes in this area shows, O'Connor's jurisprudential accommodationism influenced the collegial production of legal doctrine.

An area especially marked by a collective production of legal doctrine is civil rights policy. The contentious nature and fact-specific quality of issues such as voting rights and affirmative action have meant that split decisions have been the rule. In its civil rights cases, the contemporary Court has frequently had to focus on achieving bare plurality judgments, with the generation of doctrinal principles a distinctly secondary problem. As a result, the articulation of compromise positions often determines case outcomes. This situation seems to have accentuated O'Connor's general decisional traits of fact-based reductionism and contextual resolution of disputes; thus, her civil rights jurisprudence has been characterized by conservatively framed, context-dependent compromises that allow for the maintenance of plurality coalitions. In some cases, O'Connor has acted as the key conciliator in the production of jointly written Court opinions, and yet, despite this influence, she has yet to proffer doctrinal solutions of a lasting quality.

O'Connor's opinion writing in the civil rights area of racial discrimination in voting illustrates the above situation dramatically. The particular voting rights problem that has gripped the Court since the 1970s has been that of racial vote dilution. Vote dilution occurs when the design of electoral districts results in some votes having more influence over electoral outcomes than others. Racial abridgment of the vote comes into play when the voting strength of a racial group of voters is so affected because of patterns of racial cohesion in the electorate (Maveety 1991; Davidson 1984; Parker 1990). No definitive standards exist, however, as to what counts as evidence of vote dilution in violation of the Voting Rights Act and the Fifteenth Amendment. In the two major cases in which the contemporary Court has visited this question, the only real judicial agreement was over the case outcomes. Beyond that minimal agreement, any judicial consensus over the legal standards to be employed turned on the jurisprudential accommodationism of O'Connor.

In the 1986 decision of *Thornburgh v. Gingles* (478 U.S. 30, 1986), the Court's internal disagreement was over racial bloc voting and whether it was always coincident with racial vote dilution, identified as "the systematic frustration or exclusion of minority voters" from the process of electoral competition (Maveety 1991b, 122). This was already a contextually sensitive problem, but O'Connor did not feel that Brennan's draft opinion dealt with it contextually enough, as her conference memo to him indicated.[10] O'Connor's disagreement with Brennan concerned how to identify racially polarized voting that impairs voter choice in violation of the Voting Rights Act. Her position, articulated in one of the early drafts of her separate opinion, was that "racial bloc voting must combine with *other factors* . . . to deny minority voters an equal opportunity to participate in the political process" (second draft of 24 March 1986, pp. 11–12, Marshall Papers, box 382, folder 1 [emphasis added]). As the record of conference memos in *Gingles* shows, no fewer than three pivotal centrist justices (Powell, Stevens, and Byron White) awaited O'Connor's separate opinion before deciding their commitment to Brennan's opinion for the Court (memos of 11 and 19 February 1986, box 382, folder 1).

In the end O'Connor was successful in shaping the articulation of standards for determining vote dilution. Her critical point was that sustained proportional electoral success by a racial minority was important evidence of effective minority voting strength. In addition, she felt that district-by-district, rather than aggregate-level, statistics on minority voters' election of candidates of their choice were the critical indices (memo of 10 February 1986, Marshall Papers, box 382, folder 1). Both these evidentiary standards point toward a reductionist method of deciding voting rights cases and toward nonprogrammatic treatment of vote dilution controversies; indeed, O'Connor urged the adoption of a multifaceted "denial of fair access to the political process" standard for vote dilution claims (second draft of partial dissent/concurrence in the judgment, Marshall Papers, box 382, folder 1). A telling point is O'Connor's chief objection to Brennan's argument, highlighted by a 22 May addition to the fourth draft of her opinion: "There is no indication that Congress intended to mandate a *single, universally applicable standard* for measuring undiluted minority voting strength" (Marshall Papers, box 382, folder 2 [emphasis added]). Clearly, O'Connor objected to the use of a bright-line rule for adjudicating racial vote dilution claims.

O'Connor's concurrence in the judgment, which gained three joiners (Burger, Powell, and Rehnquist), sapped Brennan's opinion of full majority support—despite the fact that he made several significant concessions to her views[11] (see Brennan memo of 15 April 1986,

Marshall Papers, box 382, folder 1; Brennan memo of 29 May 1986 and sixth draft of opinion, Marshall Papers, box 382, folder 2). Her personal influence over doctrinal standards thus came at the expense of collegial Court authority. Her context-based, fact-driven quarrel with the Court's opinion nevertheless stressed a fundamentally conservative point: that the *Gingles* ruling should not be read to imply "the creation of a right to a form of proportional representation in favor of all geographically and politically cohesive minority groups" (106 S.Ct. at 2785).

The importance of O'Connor's contextualist position was made clear in the 1993 ruling of *Shaw v. Reno* (113 S.Ct. 2816, 1993). In *Shaw*, O'Connor's opinion for a five-justice majority rejected the unconditional appropriateness of "remedial race-based districting" implicit in Brennan's *Gingles* opinion. She argued that "racial gerrymandering," with the object of avoiding minority vote dilution and securing minority electoral influence, was just as likely to exacerbate patterns of racial bloc voting as it was to counteract them. With *Shaw*, O'Connor's apprehension regarding "racial PR" as the formula for minority political equality gained the force of precedent.

Of course, in typical O'Connor fashion, *Shaw* was a cautious ruling, deciding nothing definitively beyond the question of the claim's justiciability, but at the level of *dicta*, O'Connor engaged in the kind of discursive commentary that often characterizes her separate opinions. As with many of her concurrences, the discussion in *Shaw* was directed toward presenting her jurisprudential formulation as a position embedded in existing precedents—for example, the 1977 racial gerrymandering case of *UJO v. Carey* (430 U.S. 144, 1977). Her objective seems to have been to accommodate *Shaw* to certain strains within the Court's other civil rights decisions (see her reliance on *Wygant, Edmonson*, and *Powers*, 113 S.Ct. at 2825, 2827, and 2829). To this end, her most important argument was the repudiation of race-based districting as a categorical solution to problems of electoral and political inequality. Again, her objection was to a bright-line rule that was insufficiently sensitive to fact settings and contextual consequences.[12] It should also be noted that the jurisprudential accommodationism of her *Shaw* opinion has fairly conservative policy implications with respect to the use of race-based districting. Arguably, O'Connor's objective in *Shaw* was to try to articulate a compromise position on the relevance of racial considerations to districting fairness. This would certainly be accommodationist; whether it can guide the Court's policy making in this area awaits further litigation.

While O'Connor's jurisprudence was not as influential in shaping First Amendment doctrine, she nevertheless made distinctive contributions to the Court's jurisprudential discussions. First, she proposed a contextual method for delineating and reconciling the expressive rights of associations—the so-called "associational purpose" test (Maveety 1989). As with so much of her jurisprudential accommodationism, this test had its origin in O'Connor's separate concurrence in the 1984 case of *Roberts v. U.S. Jaycees* (468 U.S. 609, 1984). In this case, the Court upheld a state regulation requiring the Jaycees organization to end its men-only membership policy through a balancing of rights approach—in this instance, freedom of association and equal protection/nondiscrimination. O'Connor argued separately, however, that a better way to proceed was to distinguish the associational rights of expressive- versus commercial-purpose organizations (468 U.S. at 635). The associational-purpose test for associational speech rights has had some limited influence on the Court's corporate speech doctrine, and O'Connor has continued to reiterate its utility and application.[13]

Her associational-purpose test also spawned a corollary, which applied to a First Amendment problem related to associational freedom: group expression in public forums. O'Connor argued that the traditional distinction between public and nonpublic forums should be more context sensitive: rights of expressive access should turn on speaker identity and forum purpose. Speaking for a majority in 1985, O'Connor constructed a "forum-purpose" test, which holds that "control over access to a nonpublic forum can be based on subject matter and speaker identity, so long as the distinctions are *reasonable in light of the purpose served by the forum* and are viewpoint neutral" (*Cornelius v. NAACP, LDF*, 473 U.S. 788, 806 [1985]; emphasis added). O'Connor continued to apply her forum-purpose test to adjudicate organizations' First Amendment expression claims, which included two opinions that gained pluralities.[14] Generally, then, O'Connor's emphasis was on situating expressive rights claims within the context of community; this approach represented the fact-based balancing of a pragmatic centrist.[15]

This antiformulaic balancing approach is also evidenced in O'Connor's Sixth Amendment right to counsel opinions. In 1984 she authored the majority opinion in *Strickland v. Washington* (466 U.S. 668), a landmark ruling that established standards for evaluating the quality of legal representation guaranteed to criminal defendants under the Sixth Amendment. Her "reasonably effective assistance" standard called for a case-by-case analysis of whether counsel's conduct, taken in context, "undermined the proper functioning of the adversary process" (466 U.S. at 686). O'Connor's *Strickland* opinion emphasized that its principles "do not establish mechanical rules" and that the ultimate focus of inquiry must be on "the fundamental fairness of the [adversary] proceeding"[16] (466 U.S. at 696).

Her insistence on a case-by-case analysis, as well as her emphasis on a fundamental fairness approach reminiscent of Justice Felix Frankfurter, distinguishes O'Connor from the other conservatives on the Court with respect to criminal procedure matters. Her anti-bright-line approach—that "the fairness of the trial process" determined what was constitutionally requisite legal representation—is very different from a textual or a bright-line reading of the Sixth Amendment right to counsel. Her own words corroborate this assertion, as is indicated in a memo she sent to Brennan during the opinion-drafting process. In commenting on her opinion's application of the fairness standard, she observed that "it is helpful because it gives a concrete illustration of how the otherwise abstract principles articulated in the opinion apply to one particular set of facts" (memo of 13 March 1984, Marshall Papers, box 345, folder 2).

O'Connor's aversion to rigid ideological principles cuts across a broad range of constitutional issues, including those in which she is assumed to be an automatic conservative vote, such as capital punishment. Her opinions regarding capital punishment of juveniles reveal a very nonformulaic approach. In the recent juvenile death penalty cases decided by the Court, O'Connor clearly rejected both the liberal and conservative justices' ideologically driven arguments (*Thompson v. Oklahoma*, 487 U.S. 815, 857–58, 1988; *Stanford v. Kentucky*, 492 U.S. 361, 380–82, 1989). She rejected the liberals' proportionality analysis that capital punishment for anyone under the age of eighteen is always cruel and unusual; she likewise rejected the conservatives' contention that proportionality analysis is irrelevant to determining the constitutionality of capital punishment statutes applying to juveniles. O'Connor instead sought an accommodation between these two positions and based her decision on an assessment of the context (the community consensus or lack thereof) in which the juvenile death penalty statutes were devised and used. Her efforts at a compromise enkindled a somewhat nasty exchange of memos with Antonin Scalia in the first case, *Thompson v. Oklahoma*. Following O'Connor's circulation of her concurrence in the judgment to overturn the Oklahoma juvenile death penalty statute, Scalia amended his dissent with a four-and-one-half page section caustically chastising

O'Connor's "solomonic solution" (third draft of 27 June 1988, Marshall Papers, box 450, folder 7). This prompted O'Connor to send a last-minute and forcefully worded change in her opinion to the printer (memo of 28 June 1988, Marshall Papers, box 450, folder 7).

In the second case, *Stanford v. Kentucky*, O'Connor held her ground, applying her standard as articulated in *Thompson* to adjudge the Kentucky statute. While in the second case she ruled to permit capital punishment of a juvenile, she was, interestingly, on the majority side in both cases. These Eighth Amendment cases dramatically illustrate the degree to which O'Connor is independent of the ideological conservatives on the Rehnquist Court; moreover, her actions in this "law and order" area attest to the constancy with which she pursues the strategy of jurisprudential accommodationism.

Finally, in the area where it might be most tempting to characterize O'Connor's work as rule governed, formulaic, and ideologically driven as opposed to jurisprudentially accommodationist—federalism—her doctrinal positions, while almost uniformly leading to conservative states' rights results, nevertheless exhibit the use of flexible, contextually sensitive standards. In addition, her opinions in the area of judicial federalism espouse an overtly incrementalist and anti-bright-line approach. Her federalism opinions are particularly interesting in another regard: they show how her doctrinal standards can be used to appeal to both the ideological conservatives and the liberal-to-moderate members of the Court.

O'Connor's position on Tenth Amendment questions and on the powers reserved to the states under the Constitution is clearly that "federalism cannot be reduced to weak essence[s]" or "distilled" into "formal tests."[17] In the 1985 decision of *San Antonio Metropolitan Transportion Authority v. Garcia*, O'Connor was one of four dissenters objecting to the Court's application of the minimum wage and hour requirements of the Fair Labor Standards Act to municipal mass transit authority employees. Noting that it had been difficult for the Court to "craft bright line rules defining the scope of state autonomy" from federal regulation, she posited that "the proper resolution lies in *weighing* state autonomy as *a factor in the balance* when interpreting the means by which Congress can exercise its authority on the states as states" (469 U.S. 528, 588–89 [emphasis added]). Though the *Garcia* majority overruled the 1976 Burger Court precedent of *National League of Cities v. Usery* (426 U.S. 833, 1976), which articulated a balancing test for preserving the "functions essential to separate and independent existence" of states, O'Connor has persisted in her argument that the Court should carefully construe the factual circumstances of federal-state conflicts in light of "the principles of federalism implicit in the Constitution" (*South Dakota v. Baker*, 485 U.S. 505, 533–34, 1988 [O'Connor, J., dissenting]). Her more recent efforts in the Tenth Amendment area have been majority opinions, in which she has successfully defended the prerogatives of "joint sovereigns" and restored much of the *Usery* approach in carefully and contextually defined fact-based situations (quoted language is from *Gregory v. Ashcroft*, 501 U.S. 452, 458, 1991; see also *New York v. U.S.*, 112 S.Ct. 2408, 1992).

In the related area of judicial federalism—specifically, the availability of federal habeas corpus relief to state criminal defendants—O'Connor has utilized her anti-bright-line jurisprudence to signal her independence from doctrinaire approaches to federal-state court relations. For example, in *Teague v. Lane* in 1989, O'Connor spoke for a plurality holding that race-based usage of peremptory challenges could be a basis for a federal habeas corpus appeal under the Sixth Amendment but could not be applied retroactively to upset state judgments that have otherwise become final. She has not deviated from this objective of balancing fairness questions with federalism-related issues of finality in state judicial proceedings (see also *Coleman v. Thompson*, 501 U.S. 722, 1991. O'Connor majority holds that federal court respect for state criminal trials requires that federal habeas review is barred where prisoner has defaulted his federal claims in state court pursuant to an independent and adequate state procedural rule.).

Her concern for fact-based balancing of the interests of finality, federalism, and fairness has, at times, required her independence from the conservative wing of the Court, which seeks to uniformly limit federal habeas relief. In *Keeney v. Tamayo-Reyes* in 1992, she joined dissenters Blackmun, Stevens, and Kennedy in arguing that a new federal evidentiary hearing was appropriate for the district court to address a petitioner's federal habeas corpus claim, observing that no interest of federalism or comity was served by requiring the court to resolve claims based on an incomplete state court record (112 S.Ct. 1715, 1725). Similarly, she distanced herself from a "phoney federalism" concern expressed by the Court in a second 1992 habeas case, *Wright v. West*. There, she concurred in the judgment while correcting the Clarence Thomas opinion, point by point, on the standard of review for federal court review of state court applications of law to fact. As she observed in her concurrence with regard to judicial federalism:

While Justice Thomas says that we "defer" to state courts' determinations of federal law, the statement is misleading . . . [our precedents] . . . [do] not direct federal courts to spend less time or effort scrutinizing the existing federal law, on the ground that they can assume the state courts interpreted it properly. (112 S.Ct. 2482, 2497)

This statement suggests that O'Connor was objecting to Thomas's oversimplification and reduction of the habeas precedents to certain bright-line (and erroneous) principles. O'Connor's position in *Wright* and in *Keeney*, furthermore, indicates that she is willing to set aside or qualify federalism values when other interests conflict with them (see also Wermiel 1991, 140, and *Brecht v. Abrahamson*, 113 S.Ct. 1710, 1728–29, 1993 (O'Connor, J., dissenting from Court's application of "substantial and injurious effect or influence" standard to federal habeas claims of *Miranda* violations and their effect on jury verdicts).

O'Connor's espousal of a contextual jurisprudence of federal-state court relations means that critical facts, not ideological positions or coalitional loyalty, dictate her adjudication of the balance of finality and fairness interests. At times, this balance requires that she express her independence from members of her moderate conservative cohort. This was the case in the 1993 decision of *Withrow v. Williams*, in which she dissented in part from the Souter majority opinion but also remained distant from Scalia's more formulaic dissent (113 S.Ct. 1745, and at 1765, 1993). In *Withrow* the Court held that confessions that violate the *Miranda* rule are actionable rights deprivations that justify granting federal courts habeas power to overturn state convictions in which such constitutional infirmities occur. O'Connor dissented in part on the grounds that federal courts reviewing habeas petitions should apply a "totality of circumstances approach" to the question of the voluntariness of the confession and the resulting legitimacy of the conviction. She questioned the utility of *Miranda*'s supposed "bright lines" in this regard, and further observed that:

. . . the totality of circumstances approach permits *each fact to be taken into account* without resort to formal and dispositive labels. By dispensing with the difficulty of producing a yes-or-no answer to questions that are often better answered in *shades or degrees*, the voluntariness inquiry can often make judicial decision making easier rather than more onerous. It is enough that the habeas court look to the warnings or their absence, *along with all other factors*, and consider them in deciding what is, after all, the ultimate question [of the involuntariness of the confession]. (113 S.Ct. 1745, 1764 [emphasis added])

Fact-based balancing is evident in O'Connor's depiction of the correct doctrinal approach for *Miranda*-related habeas appeals; as with previous opinions, her concern is to avoid articulating blanket rules regarding federal-state court relations in the criminal trial setting. The jurisprudential accommodationism of her approach is also evident not only from the language of her opinions, but from the fact that her doctrinal positions are coincident with judicial alliances across the ideological spectrum of Rehnquist Court justices.

This initial review of O'Connor's juridical record makes certain preliminary conclusions possible. Her decisional tendency toward jurisprudential accommodationism is consistent across a range of legal issue areas and has had an impact on the Court's derivation and adoption of doctrinal standards. As has been documented, her anti-bright-line, contextually situated methods of analysis have often represented salient, viable doctrinal compromises. At a behavioral level of legal argumentation, her accommodationist style is strategic action geared toward influencing the collective production of legal policy. Her accommodationist strategy—the pragmatic centrism of her contextual conservatism—seems, moreover, to have affected the process of deriving and adopting doctrinal standards. This issue is explored further in the next chapter.

A recent revisionist account of the modern Supreme Court questions the importance attributed to centrist justices and their accommodationist legal approaches (Kahn 1994), but the evidence presented here mitigates against such a sweeping conclusion in the case of O'Connor. It is because the Supreme Court has lacked a predominant ideological or intellectual focus during O'Connor's tenure of service that her adherence to pragmatic centrism—along with an ability to be in voting alignment with the majority side in 5–4 decisions—has made her an influential justice.

In terms of her substantive contributions to the Court's policy making, O'Connor distinguishes herself most clearly in two major areas, reproductive rights and church-state conflicts, but significantly affects several other issue areas as well, yet her most distinctive contribution has been to perpetuate the balancing-of-interests approach in contemporary Supreme Court jurisprudence. While the Burger Court was often excoriated for its reliance on this jurisprudential approach (Blasi 1983; Schwartz 1987; cf. Kahn 1994 for a recent, revisionist treatment), "justices of standards" have a renewed appeal in light of Reagan's and Bush's appointment of conservative ideologues to the high bench (Sullivan 1992). O'Connor's importance in shaping constitutional policies in certain issue areas has, thus, for the time being, prevented the dominance of these areas by justices such as Scalia and Thomas with more programmatic and less flexible jurisprudential solutions.

Notes

1. Some formal theorists who examine the judiciary conceive of strategic judicial action in a game-theoretic context, that is, as the misrepresentation of preferences in order to manipulate the collective decision-making framework and achieve a desired policy outcome. Modified for the collegial court setting, strategic behavior is that which "transgresses [the judge's] own convictions *per se*, and her convictions as appropriately modified to respond to the pressures of collegial unity and sound collegial outcome" (Kornhauser and Sager 1993, 53; see also discussion, 52–55).

Murphy's classic definition of judicial strategy refers to

the overall plans under which [tactical] maneuverings against specific obstacles are coordinated and for which scarce resources are allocated in order to further the accomplishment of broad policy goals (Murphy 1964, 9–10).

2. The neo-institutionalists would also deny that judicial ideology or personal attitudes fully determine judicial choice. Neo-institutionalist judicial scholars posit that a court's institutional arrangements, including internal and external rules, organizational structure, and structural context, condition the aggregation of individual preferences within the decision-making body (Brace and Hall 1993, 916; Smith 1988). Although they emphasize different independent or explanatory variables, neo-institutionalist and small group proponents stress that judicial decisions are the result of a complex interaction of attitudinal preferences, decisional rules and context, and group structure and dynamics. See also Murphy's (1964) extended discussion of tactics of influence—all of which presume that justices view each other in terms of fluidity.

3. This is even more true when the conservatives are divided into "academic conservative" and "pragmatic conservative" blocs. For example, a justice like Antonin Scalia, whose free-market conservatism is animated by the law and economics school of scholarship and whose professional background includes academic service, exhibits a categorical and philosophically inspired brand of judicial conservatism, which he combines with a fairly noncollegial interpretation of the role of the judge on multimember courts. The same might be said for Justice Clarence Thomas's natural-law-inspired conservatism, wherein a judicial ideology is deduced from philosophical first principles. Conversely, a justice like O'Connor, whose conservatism springs from party politics and a professional background of political bargaining over policy

objectives, exhibits a less stringently rule-governed conservatism, one that is highly fact and context sensitive and one that is driven by the need for flexible interpretation of authoritative legal documents, instead of by a derivation from ideological principles. The distinctive nature of O'Connor's conservatism consists of her use of

> particular doctrinal test[s] to indicate . . . what the proper role of a judge is—how much of a judge's own perceptions and values can be injected in constitutional adjudication. And again, I suggest that, in this area, her approach separates her from what would be the perceived model of a conservative judge ("Symposium" 1991, 143).

The very nature of O'Connor's pragmatic conservatism requires a more bargaining- and compromise-oriented, cooperative conception of the decision-making enterprise of collegial courts.

    4. For example, until her plurality opinion in *Planned Parenthood v. Casey* (112 S.Ct. 2791, 1992), her opinions in the abortion area had been evenly split between concurrences and dissents. Regardless of her alignment with either the winning or losing side in an abortion case, O'Connor was clearly inclined to express her distinctive thoughts on the matter.

    This is similarly true in an area in which O'Connor is thought to be less independent: judicial federalism. While she is generally in agreement with court majorities (or perhaps they are in agreement with her), she is not above using separate opinions to signal her disagreement with certain doctrinal positions as well as with certain judicial coalitions. See *Brecht v. Abrahamson*, 113 S.Ct. 1710, 1728 (1993)(O'Connor, J., dissenting); *Withrow v. Williams*, 113 S.Ct. 1745, 1756 (1993)(O'Connor, J., partial dissent); *Keeney v. Tamayo-Reyes*, 112 S.Ct. 1715, 1725 (1992)(O'Connor, J., dissenting).

    5. The second draft of O'Connor's dissenting opinion commented that the solicitor general's brief for *Akron* urged the adoption of an "unduly burdensome" test to adjudicate reproductive rights claims (Marshall Papers, box 314, folder 11, pp. 14–15, n. 10).

    6. See the first draft of her dissenting opinion in *Thornburgh v. American College of Obstetricians* (1986) (Marshall Papers, box 382, folder 6, pp. 15–16).

    7. See Cameron 1993, 43ff, on the role of the "fact-to-outcome function" in judicial decision making.

    8. A subsequent O'Connor concurrence, in the 1990 parental notification abortion decision of *Hodgson v. Minnesota*, reiterated the "unduly burdens" test and applied it to uphold a two-parent notification requirement with a judicial bypass option for minors seeking abortions (497 U.S. 417, 458–60 [1990]; 110 S.Ct. 2926, 2949–50, 1990). The Court itself was fractured into a plurality over the issue, but interestingly, O'Connor read her test into Stevens's plurality opinion and his discussion of "unreasonable obstacles" (497 U.S. at 459; 110 S.Ct. at 2949–50, citing 110 S.Ct. at 2937). Despite the similarity in language, the Court did not formally adopt the O'Connor approach.

9. The test originated in the 1971 ruling of *Lemon v. Kurtzman* and provided a three-part analysis of government involvement in religion and with religious institutions. To survive First Amendment scrutiny, governmental conduct must (1) have a secular purpose, (2) have a primary effect of neither advancing nor inhibiting religion, and (3) avoid excessive entanglement between the state and religious bodies.

10. O'Connor urged the introduction of an additional factual dimension to the question of what was dilutionary, racially polarized voting. Her comment was that she was "not persuaded that Congress intended that districts in which a very large minority of white voters frequently vote for black candidates should be treated as exhibiting racial bloc voting as your opinion seems to imply" (memo of 10 February 1986, Marshall Papers, box 382, folder 1). In other words, she questioned the assumption that the help of white voters in electing a minority-selected candidate meant that such a candidate was not really preferred or chosen by minority voters.

11. Both White and Stevens wrote separate opinions concurring and dissenting in part; White also signaled his agreement with O'Connor. Significantly, Brennan's concessions to O'Connor caused Marshall to defect from part of Brennan's opinion; he instead joined part of Stevens's separate dissent.

12. More broadly, she speculated that racial gerrymandering "threatens special harms" that are distinct from the dilution of a racial group's voting strength (113 S.Ct. at 2828). The harms she had in mind were stigmatic and separationist; "racial balkanization" was the potential consequence of the reliance on race-based categorizations in the electoral context (113 S.Ct. at 2828, 2832). The implications of this view for the remedial use of race-based classifications in civil rights policy generally are obvious. O'Connor's efforts to generate a single standard for adjudging racial classifications in civil rights controversies is explored further in chapter 7.

13. See her majority opinion in *Massachusetts Citizens for Life v. FEC*, 479 U.S. 238 (1986), and *New York State Club Association v. NYC*, 487 U.S. 1 (1988). For corollary extensions of the test, see her dissenting opinions in *Rust v. Sullivan*, 500 U.S. 173, 223, (1991), and *Bray v. Alexandria Women's Health Clinic*, 113 S.Ct. 753, 799, (1993). See also Rehnquist's unanimous opinion in *Keller v. State Board of California*, 496 U.S. 1,4 (1990).

14. *Boos v. Barry*, 485 U.S. 312, 1988; *U.S. v. Kokinda*, 497 U.S. 720, 1990. In *U.S. v. Kokinda*, O'Connor's forum-purpose rationale for regulation of postal solicitation was instrumental in converting her dissenting draft opinion into a judgment of the Court (see Marshall Papers, box 505, folder 8). See also the 1992 case, *International Society for Krishna Consciousness v. Lee*, 112 S.Ct. 2701, in which O'Connor concurs in partial restriction of forum use based on forum purpose (permitting leafleting but not solicitation in airport terminal facility).

15. A recent article on public forum doctrine defends a "categorical analysis approach" and argues that the current Court must delineate "the analytical

tier between broad theory and narrow doctrine'' (BeVier 1992, 122). The argument of this chapter is that O'Connor's use of categories of forums aims to do this.

16. O'Connor's fact-based, reductionist approach animated not only her later majority opinion in *Satterwhite v. Texas* (486 U.S. 249, at 256, 1988), but also Stevens's opinion for the Court in *Penson v. Ohio* (488 U.S. 75, 77 [1988]; 109 S.Ct. 346, at 353–54, 1988).

17. The above language comes from her dissents in *San Antonio Metropolitan Transportation Authority v. Garcia*, 469 U.S. 528, 580 (1985), and *South Carolina v. Baker*, 485 U.S. 505, 533 (1988).

Chapter Four

The Juridical Record: Behavioral Accommodationism

The previous chapter surveyed the O'Connor juridical record for evidence of her jurisprudential accommodationism. In this chapter, the same juridical record is examined from a more behavioral perspective. As mentioned in the previous chapter, O'Connor's judicial accommodationism has both a jurisprudential and a behavioral dimension. Two distinct yet interdependent decisional tendencies make up O'Connor's behavioral accommodationism: her propensity for majority-side membership and her pursuit of the alternative leadership tactic of concurring opinion writing. As this chapter shows, these coalitional behaviors complement the jurisprudential accommodationism profiled in chapter 3.

Phase 1: Alliance with a Winning Coalition

O'Connor's pragmatic centrism arguably reflects her experiences as a majority leader in the Arizona senate. In that capacity, O'Connor had to reconcile divergent points of view in order to achieve passage of various pieces of legislation. In her attempts to secure passage for different legislative initiatives, O'Connor no doubt appreciated the importance of majority-side membership for wielding influence or leadership and the value of compromise to achieve results. Once on the Burger Court, O'Connor realized that a rigid adherence to an inflexible ideological philosophy—of either a conservative or liberal persuasion—would not be conducive to maximizing her influence on the Court. Particularly in close cases, a pragmatic centrist ideology that incorporates a willingness to shift position based on facts would be useful in consistently becoming part of a majority coalition.

Examination of Table 4.1 illustrates O'Connor's aptitude for becoming a member of the Court's majority side, regardless of its ideological composition[1]. For all of her terms on the Court for which case statistics are available, O'Connor was a member of the five-justice majority in well over half of the 5–4 decisions made, with the exceptions of her 1981 and her 1992 terms on the Court. Despite her predisposition to vote in an overall conservative direction, O'Connor clearly exhibited a tendency during her service on the Burger Court (1981 to 1985 terms) to join a five-justice majority coalition that was not composed solely of conservatives. (Of course, the reality of the Burger Court was its lack of a predominating and enduring conservative majority coalition, despite the many GOP appointees.) This tendency is strikingly illustrated in the 1985 term, which was Burger's last as Chief Justice:

TABLE 4.1
O'Connor's Voting Behavior in 5–4 Decisions: 1981–1993

Court Term	% of time O'Connor was part of 5-justice majority	% of time O'Connor was part of 5-justice conservative majority
1981	41.9%	38.5%[a]
1982	63.6	57.1
1983	60.7	52.9
1984	52.6	40.0
1985	83.3	43.3
1986	57.7	69.2[b]
1987	66.6	87.5[c]
1988	75.7	76.0
1989	69.2	66.7
1990	71.4	42.8[d]
1991	57.1	14.3[e]
1992	44.4	27.7[f]

a. Conservative alliance: Burger, White, Rehnquist, Powell, O'Connor.
b. Conservative alliance: White, Rehnquist, Powell, O'Connor, Scalia.
c. Conservative alliance: White, Rehnquist, O'Connor, Scalia, Kennedy.
d. Conservative alliance: White, Rehnquist, O'Connor, Scalia, Kennedy, Souter.
e. Conservative alliance: White, Rehnquist, O'Connor, Scalia, Kennedy, Souter, Thomas. O'Connor most often acted with the ideologically mixed judicial alliance of Blackmun, Stevens, Kennedy, and Souter.
f. The most frequent five-justice alliance during this term was Rehnquist, White, Scalia, Kennedy, and Thomas.

O'Connor was on the majority side in more than 83 percent of the 5–4 decisions, yet conservatives constituted the entire majority coalition in only 43 percent of those decisions.

After Rehnquist became Chief Justice in the 1986 term, O'Connor maintained her propensity to be on the majority side in 5–4 decisions but increased her fealty to the conservative alliance. With the addition of Scalia and the subsequent replacement of Powell by Kennedy, the number of consistent conservatives on the Court increased significantly. The conservatives were thus in a dominant position with respect to 5-4 Court splits. Perhaps cognizant of a shift in power from a centrist group of Burger Court justices to a conservative bloc of Rehnquist Court justices, O'Connor accordingly changed her alignment strategy in 5–4 decisions. The percentage of cases in which O'Connor was part of a five-justice majority composed solely of conservatives greatly increased from 1986 to 1989.

This percentage remained at a very high level until the 1990–1992 terms. While O'Connor still frequently acts as a member of five-justice majorities, her partners in alliance seem to be changing. For instance, during the 1991 term O'Connor acted most often in 5-justice majorities with the mixed alliance of Blackmun, Stevens, Souter, and Kennedy. By the time of the October 1992 term, O'Connor was no longer a critical or prevalent member of either a 5–4 majority or a 5–4 conservative alliance. Whether this behavior indicates a change in O'Connor or a change in the conservative bloc with which she once identified is unclear. What is clear, however, is that while the relative proportion of 5–4 decisions was fairly constant over time, the size of the conservative alliance (or protoalliance) had increased by the 1991 term to include more than five justices.

Along with this general propensity for majority-side membership, O'Connor also behaves with what might be called strategic fluidity. In other words, her coalitional position remains flexible, often until the ultimate moment of decision. Even a cursory examination of the record found in the Thurgood Marshall Papers reveals that O'Connor both changes her conference votes and delays her commitment to the Court's circulated opinions. These behaviors were in evidence, for example, in both *Webster* and *Allegheny*, discussed in the previous chapter. Another instance of strategic fluidity occurred in the *Thompson* capital punishment case, as this memo from O'Connor to Stevens indicates: "This is a difficult case for me. I am still not at rest on it and will not make a final decision until I see the dissenting opinion" (memo of 22 January 1988, Marshall Papers, box 450, folder 8). O'Connor sent a similar memo to the Chief Justice in the more minor criminal procedure case of *Powers v. Ohio* (499 U.S. 400, 1991):

> My vote at Conference was very tentative. I plan to see what Tony [Kennedy] writes and decide whether I can join it. Is it all right with you if we defer assignment of this dissent? (see the memo of 16 October 1990, Marshall Papers, box 524, folder 3)

While O'Connor is by no means the only justice to engage in strategic fluidity, her mutability seems to be a fairly regular occurrence and often has important consequences for opinion assignment and support.[2] She is also amenable to signaling conditional agreement as leverage to induce compromise in opinion language that would permit fuller agreement, as the record of conference memos in the 1986 affirmative action case of *Johnson v. Transportation Agency* and the 1986 voting rights case of *Thornburgh v. Gingles* shows.[3] A very dramatic instance of this type of strategic action occurred in the 1989 civil rights case of *Price Waterhouse v. Hopkins*, in which a significant amount of collaborative exchange ensued between Brennan, writing for the Court, and O'Connor, threatening to concur in the judgment. (In the end, Brennan's opinion gained only a plurality [Marshall Papers, box 471, folders 3 and 4].)

While the above empirical evidence is far from systematic, it indicates a sensitivity on O'Connor's part to her place in the Court's coalitional arrangements. Her decisional tendency of behavioral accommodation is thus tempered by a certain amount of shrewdness. This is perhaps because her majority-side membership is often in the judgment alone or through the vehicle of the separate concurrence.

Phase 2: The Concurring Strategy

As observed at this chapter's outset, there are two facets to O'Connor's behavioral accommodationism: majority-side alliance and strategic use of separate opinions. These behavioral tendencies work in tandem and result in the juridical position that is labeled pragmatic centrism. The dynamics of the latter behavior—separate opinion writing—are, however, much less well understood than other aspects of judicial coalition formation.

While judicial scholars have made much progress in correlating judicial attitudes, ideology, and votes (see, e.g., Hagle and Spaeth

1992), their understanding of judicial opinions is less sophisticated. While some studies using small group analysis have offered testable hypotheses about judicial decision-making and coalition formation on multimember courts (Howard 1968; Ulmer 1971; Rohde 1972; Brenner 1989; Winkle and Axelrod 1992), little work has directly addressed opinion production. Specifically, neither political science nor legal literatures have adequately explained the issuance of separate opinions by judges on collegial courts.

Of separate opinions, those that most defy understanding are *concurrences*. Dissents are intuitively more comprehensible—they register disagreement, both with the outcome and the legal reasoning of the court majority—but concurrences are neither complete disagreement nor agreement; as opinions, they either annotate majority opinions or offer alternative doctrinal analyses (Ray 1990, 780–81; Kornhauser and Sager 1993, 8, n. 14). Given the workload demands of the Supreme Court, why would justices devote time and energy to writing opinions in cases where they agree with the decision reflected in the majority opinion—an opinion which, according to numerous small group studies, they helped to formulate?

The traditional answer to this question relies on the so-called judicial ego thesis. According to this view, concurring opinions are a function of intellectual egotism, lack of judicial restraint, and defiance of norms of consensuality (Peterson 1981). As individual excrescences, concurring opinions have no legal impact, that is, they are not opinions of the Court. Of course, these same features render concurring opinions very significant from a behavioral perspective, as individualized expressions reflecting the attitudes, values, and ideologies of justices. Such opinions may indeed be more revealing than justices' majority opinions, which are products of group processes involving conciliation and compromise. Concurring opinions are thus useful indicators of strong feelings on an issue and reveal much about the actual attitude of a justice (Riggs 1983; Kelman 1986; Kornhauser and Sager 1993, 9). Content analysis of separate opinions, then, offers the potential for greater insight into the prevailing belief patterns and decisional criteria of the justices.

Such analysis, moreover, might foster meaningful distinctions between justices of similar ideological beliefs. Apart from noting differences in the strength of a particularly held ideology, judicial process studies generally have not produced empirically distinctive categories for justices who possess a similar ideological disposition, for example, liberal, moderate, or conservative; yet analysis of the current Court shows the inadequacy of employing the descriptor "conservative" in a unidimensional fashion. For example, the recent abortion decisions reveal that serious fissures exist within the conservative bloc of justices of the Rehnquist Court. Attention to the concurring opinions that frequently bracket the rulings of the Court could shed light on the nature of the fissures within Rehnquist Court coalitions.[4]

Beyond this descriptive assessment of the relative import of concurring opinions, more specific reasons exist to support systematic analysis of the occurrence of concurrence. Consider the following proposition:

> the concurrence, with more authority than the dissent, may propose future avenues for development of the law laid down by the majority . . . and is both an agent of stare decisis and an agent of change. (Ray 1990, 783)

Hence, concurrence can be seen as integral to the judicial decision-making dynamic. As such, it is not simply judicial spleen venting, but strategic action to influence collective outcomes. Empirical evidence lends credence to this assertion.

Of principal importance is the fact that concurrences are an aspect of the identified "demise in consensual norms" on the modern Supreme Court (Walker, Epstein, and Dixon 1988; Haynie 1989; Witt 1986). Since the early 1940s, the justices have increasingly filed separate opinions, including both dissents and concurrences (Walker, Epstein, and Dixon 1988, 362–63). This "demise in consensual norms" has been linked to the leadership style of Chief Justice Harlan Fiske Stone (Walker, Epstein, and Dixon 1988, 384). As Chief Justice, Stone declined to use his powers to foster consensus on the Court; the result was higher rates of dissensus, as associate justices felt freer to express their individual thoughts in concurring and dissenting opinions. Separate opinions were no longer aberrations, but became increasingly common, providing a focal point for the behavioral orientation of judicial studies. Scholars identified patterns of behavior with regard to separate opinions, but their analyses generally focused on the vote component of separate opinion writing and so concentrated almost exclusively on dissents. As a result, little analysis of separate opinion writing addressed the actual opinion facet of concurrences.[5]

If the Stone leadership style and the ensuing erosion of consensual norms have continued, though, this facet of concurring opinions may be of considerable importance. Concurrence could plausibly represent an alternative avenue for leadership or influence under conditions of nonconsensuality. Concurrence is conditional agreement that does not immediately jeopardize even a minimum winning coalition; indeed, "concurring opinions take account of and respect the link between majority judgment and collective court authority" (Kornhauser and Sager 1993, 9). In effect, concurrence free rides on an existing coalitional agreement while signaling decisional or jurisprudential conditions on future agreement. The concurring opinion, then, is a way of presenting options to ideological cohorts, none of whom is bound by a stringent norm of consensus (Maveety 1991a). The concurring position is thus a strategic behavior on the part of justices, a behavior whose importance as a leadership tactic is magnified by the decline of consensual norms and the resultant lack of strong institutional role expectations on the Court.

Concurrence is both an aspect of and a factor contributing to judicial fluidity. Its occurrence challenges both attitudinal and role-based notions of judicial cooperation. Judicial behaviorists may debate about whether attitudinal consensus or allegiance to institutional norms produces stability in judicial coalitions (Winkle and Axelrod 1992; Baum 1992; Hagle and Spaeth 1991; Brenner and Spaeth 1990b; Spaeth and Altfeld 1985a; Brenner 1989), but the concurring strategy suggests that judicial cohesion is—as traditional legal theory has long held—a matter of persuasive legal argument (Epstein and Kobylka 1992; for a somewhat antagonistic presentation of the legal model of judicial action, see Segal and Spaeth 1993). Presumably, then, concurring behavior has an effect on both coalition destabilization and formation (Schwartz 1992, 241)—it induces as well as evidences fluidity. Concurrence could therefore be considered a rational strategy for judicial actors seeking to influence the future formation and composition of winning opinion coalitions.

Concurring opinions are distinct messages in intercourt communication: they can be signals to lower courts about alternative legal formulations of an issue or a strategy for limiting the scope of the majority's reasoning (Kelman 1986; Kornhauser and Sager 1993, 9). Like dissents, then, concurrences may be "damage control mechanisms" that attempt to alter and shape the future direction of the law (quoted language is from Brennan 1986, 430). "Damage control" refers to a judge's effort to constrain the application of a ruling by the Court by going on the record with his or her principled objections or qualifications. Such damage control becomes especially operative when the concurror is a critical fifth vote limiting a foundational decision

(Kelman 1986). The legal effectuality of a concurring opinion, thus, is not unrelated to the retention of majority-side membership. This is the case whether the opinion is a special concurrence, joining only the Court's disposition of a case and offering a separate rationale for decision, or a regular concurrence, joining the Court's opinion in its entirety but offering a separate commentary on its interpretation.[6]

O'Connor's behavior clearly confirms that concurring opinions can be legally influential while lacking the precedental value of an opinion for the Court. Her use of the concurring strategy is well documented: the legal literature remarks repeatedly on her tendency to use concurring opinions to send doctrinal messages to judicial colleagues and future litigants (Riggs 1983; Note 1985b; Wohl 1989; Taylor 1989; Feder 1988). As previously observed, in two legal areas—church-state conflicts and abortion rights—she has been successful in using concurrence to signal that the issue remained in dispute and to create opportunities for reconsideration of the "official doctrinal position" (see Epstein and Kobylka, 1992). Arguably, her opinion-writing behaviors strongly suggest that the demise of consensual norms on the Court has meant the emergence of new leadership tactics and of a new norm of collegial decision-making. In any case, O'Connor illustrates the strategy of the swing justice in the Rehnquist era: alignment that alternates between a moderate conservative and an ultraconservative coalition.

Because the concurring strategy is one of accommodation, it also coincides with her anti-bright-line reasoning and situational approach to jurisprudential rule making. The previous chapter noted O'Connor's aversion to bright-line reasoning: she eschews formulaic solutions to constitutional policy problems. Anti-bright-line reasoning entails a predilection for contextual or situational analyses of legal questions, as well as case-by-case balancing of competing rights claims (Gelfand and Werhan 1990; Sherry 1986; Feder 1988; Taylor 1989; Maveety and Bradley 1993). Both the concurring strategy and anti-bright-line reasoning are consistent with a justice who views her influence on the Court in terms of pragmatic centrism.[7]

To assess the validity of treating concurring opinion writing as a feature of O'Connor's behavioral accommodationism, a comparison must first be made between the issuance of concurring opinions by Justice O'Connor and her contemporaries on the Court. Figure 1 displays the separate opinion writing tendencies of ten recent Supreme Court justices.[8] The clear bar in the graph represents for each justice the percentage of written concurring opinions filed based on the ratio

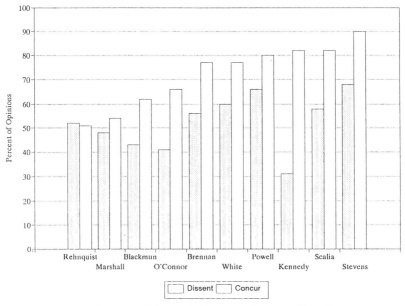

Fig. 1. Separate Opinions Written per Separate Vote Cast

of the total number of authored concurring opinions over the total number of concurrences.[9] For comparative purposes, the shaded bar in the graph represents for each justice the percentage of written dissenting opinions filed based on the ratio of the total number of authored dissenting opinions over the total number of dissents.

Analysis of figure 1 reveals variation in the separate opinion-writing behaviors of the justices. In figure 1, the justices are arrayed according to the percentage of concurring opinions they filed. Generally, the justices of this period are more prone to author concurring than dissenting opinions, per concurring or dissenting vote cast. (In fact, the only justice who does not fit that pattern is Rehnquist, who had a slightly higher percentage of dissenting than concurring opinions.) O'Connor's separate opinion-writing tendencies reflect the common judicial tendency of writing a higher percentage of concurring than dissenting opinions. O'Connor wrote concurring opinions for 66 percent of the concurring votes she cast and wrote dissenting opinions for 41 percent of the dissenting votes she cast. The difference for O'Connor between these percentages is the second highest among the justices, surpassed only by the difference for Kennedy, yet O'Connor's concurring opinion-writing proclivity, generally, is surpassed by a majority of the justices shown in the graph.

Figure 2 reveals the variation over time in O'Connor's separate opinion-writing behavior.[10] The percentage of concurring opinions per concurrence by O'Connor ranges from a high of 86 percent in 1985 to a low of 27 percent in 1988. These data suggest that the collective concurring strategy is, at times, just as important for O'Connor as the individual concurring opinion-writing strategy. Additionally of note, the percentage of dissenting opinions exceeds the percentage of concurring opinions in the last year included in the graph (1989). It is interesting to note that O'Connor's propensity to express herself in dissent sharply increased in 1989, when the conservative justices were thought to be in virtual control of the Court. Perhaps this is a further indication of the fissures that exist among the conservative bloc, and of O'Connor's desire to be independent of that bloc.

In examining O'Connor's concurring opinion-writing tendencies in terms of her aggregate opinion output, her concurring opinions account for about 25 percent of her lifetime total opinion output. Table 4.2 puts this figure in perspective by comparing it with the Court average for the terms of O'Connor's tenure of service.[11] The frequency and distribution of O'Connor's opinion writing for the total of written

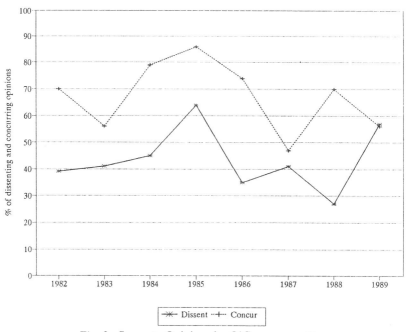

Fig. 2. Separate Opinions by O'Connor, per Year

TABLE 4.2
O'Connor's Written Opinions: 1981–1993

Term	1981				1982				1983			
	O	C	D	T	O	C	D	T	O	C	D	T
O'Connor	13	12	10	35	16	7	11	34	17	10	9	36
Average	15.7	10.5	15	41.2	16.8	7.7	15.5	40.1	16.8	7.5	14.1	38.4

Term	1984				1985				1986			
	O	C	D	T	O	C	D	T	O	C	D	T
O'Connor	16	11	9	36	17	12	7	36	18	11	13	42
Average	15.4	6.8	17.8	35.3	16.2	9.8	17.8	44	16.1	8.4	17.1	41.7

Term	1987				1988				1989			
	O	C	D	T	O	C	D	T	O	C	D	T
O'Connor	16	8	12	36	13	12	8	33	17	7	5	29
Average	15.2	7.1	10.7	33.1	14.8	9.7	12.8	37.4	14.6	9.4	13.1	37.1

Term	1990				1991				1992			
	O	C	D	T	O	C	D	T	O	C	D	T
O'Connor	16	4	5	25	15	11	11	37	13	7	11	31
Average	13.3	5.2	10.5	29.1	12.8	8.3	9.8	31	11.9	7	9	27.9

O = Opinions of the Court (includes majority and plurality opinions)
C = Concurring opinions
D = Dissenting opinions
T = Total written opinions

opinions seems fairly consistent across terms, but O'Connor did write an above-average number of concurring opinions for several of the terms shown in table 4.2. Clearly, concurring opinion writing is not a behavior that is alien to O'Connor; moreover, in the 1991 and 1992 terms she wrote an above-average number of dissenting opinions, matching or exceeding her concurring opinion-writing rates.

Speculation based on aggregate voting data, however, can go only so far. Measures of court leadership must be sensitive to qualitative as well as quantitative evidentiary factors, but a critical substantive problem in any discussion of intra-Court dynamics is how to define a "court leader." Most definitions originate in the small group approach to describing the Supreme Court's decision-making. A classic, early small group study of judicial leadership and group structure posited that collegial courts allow certain judges to exercise leadership through opinion initiation and support (Murphy 1966). This position found support in Howard's observation (1968) of the fluidity of judicial choice on the Court. In certain cases, Howard demonstrated that the interaction among justices was sufficient for some of them to change their initial decisions about the cases. A more recent commentator concluded that "a Court may have patterns of influence that give special weight to the positions of some justices in determining the Court's policies" (Baum 1989, 150).

The institutional prominence of the Chief Justice has meant a scholarly preoccupation with his or her leadership role (Steamer 1986; Davis 1990); indeed, two key tools of influence used by the Chief Justice—opinion assignment and directing conference discussion—are specifically powers of that office, and these tools/powers have become the foundation for the conceptualization of social and task leadership. According to David J. Danelski, the author of this typology, a social leader maintains favorable social and emotional conditions on the Court, while a task leader directs the Court to the successful completion of its decision of cases (Danelski 1968, 151–52). In subsequent work, Danelski argued that any member of the Court could be a social and/or task leader (Danelski 1973) and that what accounts for patterns of influence is that certain justices are social or task leaders with more regularity than their colleagues (Danelski and Danelski 1989). In expanding the leadership typology to include associate justices, however, the social and task leader roles may themselves require redefinition. Leadership behavior by associate justices, by definition, includes other tools of influence and extend beyond the existing role typology.

Leadership is best understood in terms of influence. Influence can be wielded through a variety of Court actions that justices perform, such as conference discussion, voting, memo circulation, and opinion writing. Influence implies direct interaction between justices—where one justice responds to the activity of another justice (Danelski 1968). Other small group research confirms that the most active member of a judicial subgroup is likely to wield the greatest influence in the subgroup (Ulmer 1971). Opinion initiation is, therefore, a viable indicator of justices' activity on the Court. To be considered influential, a justice must then initiate a significant number of opinions and experience a significant degree of support for those opinions (Altfeld and Spaeth 1984; Spaeth and Altfeld 1985a).

Such support need not be instantaneous to be significant, and so such opinions could include concurrences.[12] While most small group studies do not address them, their potential importance in collegial, doctrinal policy making is real, if somewhat understated. Clearly, the concurring position can be strategic, because it can be pivotal to present and future case outcomes, as well as critical to the balancing of interests that facilitates coalition building and subsequently shapes constitutional policy making (Blasi 1983; O'Brien 1990; Ginsburg 1990). In these ways, it differs from a dissenting vote in both its strategy and its impact.

Obviously, a concurrence becomes especially significant if its reasoning garners majority support in subsequent cases. (This is the long-term goal, or payoff, of the concurring strategy.) The author of the concurrence would be exerting a kind of leadership, in that his or her separate opinion would be influencing the Court's development of doctrine. It is, moreover, a tactic of influence that permits both alliance with the winning coalition and assertion of one's own distinctive legal reasoning (Maveety 1991a; Rohde 1972).

Such influence cannot be subsumed under the task or social leader role, as it represents a somewhat oblique leadership device; indeed, certain Court commentators remain unconvinced that concurrence is a useful influence tactic, as the costs of its use are allegedly high. Commentators adhering to this view often single out O'Connor as an exemplary illustration. After noting the frequency with which O'Connor files concurrences as addenda to opinions of the Court, a 1993 study observes that:

> O'Connor . . . was among the worst offenders in precluding formation of majority opinion coalitions. Her unwillingness to yield when others were assigned to write the opinion of the Court may have exacerbated the intransigence of those who specially concurred when she was assigned the opinion of the Court. (Segal and Spaeth 1993, 294–95)

If separate opinion writing is susceptible to this "tit-for-tat" behavior (Axelrod 1970), then the issuance of separate opinions—particularly concurrences—should somehow undermine the norm of "collegial agency" under which the Court operates.[13] If this is the case, it is hard to explain why some of O'Connor's concurring arguments later find support among her colleagues.

An equally plausible hypothesis is that separate opinions serve functions consistent with a collegial understanding of the Court. Along these lines, another 1993 study asserts that

the opportunity for challenge and response afforded by the publication of dissenting and concurring opinions is a close and sympathetic neighbor of the obligation of reasoned justification.[14] (Kornhauser and Sager 1993, 9)

Arguably, then, concurrence cannot be dismissed as a tool of influence, particularly where no stable, winning coalition of justices exists or where only a fragile, minimum winning coalition exists (Maveety 1991a). The instability or fragility of either coalition turns on the ideological or jurisprudential cohesiveness of the coalition members; where this is in question, the coalition is not firm and its doctrinal direction is uncertain.[15] In this situation, the utility of concurrence is that it offers an alternative position for the settlement of future cases and, hypothetically, for the establishment of a more permanent winning coalition.

By documenting the incidence of O'Connor's concurring opinions and then identifying the doctrinal messages of those opinions, we can ascertain whether her concurrences served these purposes.

As discussed previously, in the area of reproductive freedom, O'Connor's concurring voice articulated an alternative test for adjudging the abrogation of abortion rights. Rather than alienating her from the Court, her issuance of separate opinions, combined with her pivotal position on the issue, accentuated her jurisprudential influence. O'Connor's now-familiar standard—first announced in a dissent—is that a state regulation must "*unduly burden*" a woman in her right to choose abortion before heightened scrutiny of it will be employed by the reviewing court (*Akron v. Akron Center for Reproductive Health*, 462 U.S. 416, 461, 1983). O'Connor's approach hardly leads to radical results, as her concurring opinion in the recent abortion case of *Webster v. Reproductive Health Services* (1989) shows. O'Connor's action preserved the *Roe* precedent, but her application of the "unduly burdens" test upheld Missouri's restrictions on abortions, including the controversial viability testing during the first trimester. Likewise, in the 1990 parental notification-abortion decision of *Hodgson v. Minnesota*, she reiterated the "unduly burdens" test in concurrence and applied it to uphold a two-parent notification requirement with a judicial bypass option for minors seeking abortions (497 U.S. 417, 458; 110 S.Ct. 2926, 2949–50, 1990).

In *Hodgson* the Court was fractured into a plurality over the issue; interestingly, O'Connor read her test into Stevens's plurality opinion and his discussion of "unreasonable obstacles" (497 U.S. at 436; 110 S.Ct. at 2949–50, citing 110 S.Ct. at 2937). Similarly, in *Webster*, the year before, her "unduly burdens" formulation was not specifically adopted by the Court, despite her pivotal concurring vote; nevertheless, Blackmun's partial concurrence in *Webster* alluded favorably to her test (492 U.S. 490, 545, n. 6; Note 1989), signaling its growing acceptance as the position of moderate compromise. Finally, in *Planned Parenthood v. Casey* in 1992, O'Connor wrote a plurality opinion that formally presented the "unduly burdens" test as the appropriate standard for assessing governmental restrictions on abortion (112 S.Ct. 2791, 1992). While her opinion was joined in full by only Souter and Kennedy, her position has become the official alternative to *Roe*'s trimester framework for the settlement of future cases.

With respect to First Amendment church-state jurisprudence, evidence of O'Connor's impact is even more dramatic. Approximately half of her opinions in this area have been clarificatory concurrences. As previously discussed, her major contribution was a new approach for adjudicating church-state relations. The accepted approach to establishment clause problems had been the tripartite *Lemon* test, which originated in a Burger Court ruling of the early 1970s. Almost since its inception, the *Lemon* test had been subject to criticism by the justices and legal scholars because of its complexity and imprecision (Kelman 1986; Levy 1986).

O'Connor's criticism of *Lemon* came in her concurrence in the 1984 decision of *Lynch v. Donnelly*, the first case to uphold a city's Christmastime nativity display. Her criticism of the *Lemon* test was nothing new; what was new was her proposal to replace it with an "endorsement of religion" standard. Her approach rejected the utility of the various prongs of the *Lemon* test; instead, it asked simply whether a governmental action conveys a message of endorsement or disapproval of a religion or religions (465 U.S. 668, 687). In distinction to *Lemon*'s allegedly "high wall of separation" of church and state, O'Connor's accommodationist approach did not preclude government from taking religion into account in making public policy.

The endorsement test has been explicitly acknowledged as a viable analytic formula and employed by other justices in several subsequent decisions on establishment clause issues.[16] O'Connor's test was also the target of direct and specific attack by another justice, who objected to its growing doctrinal influence, particularly because of its diminished precedental value as the creation of a *concurring* opinion. Dissenting from the second crèche decision in *Allegheny v. ACLU*, Kennedy blamed the "bizarre result" in the case on the Court's employment of O'Connor's endorsement test and argued vehemently that "it has never been [understood] that a concurring opinion suggesting a clarification of our doctrine should take precedence over an opinion joined by the Court" (492 U.S. 573, 641). If specific and purposeful attack is an indirect acknowledgment of a doctrine's influence and importance, O'Connor's endorsement test certainly qualifies in the wake of Kennedy's lambasting.

Her persistent discussion of the test in successive concurrences since 1984[17] attests to a particular kind of doctrinal leadership, that of the key conciliator in a fragile but controlling coalition. It is arguable that a permanent winning coalition has already coalesced around the flexible and religiously accommodationist endorsement approach. In the 1993 ruling of *Lamb's Chapel v. Center Moriches Union Free School District* (113 S.Ct. 2141, 1993), the Court unanimously approved the after-hours use of public school facilities for the public screening of a film with a Christian perspective on family values. The language of the endorsement test infected White's opinion for the Court, as well as Kennedy's and Scalia's separate concurrences (113 S.Ct. at 2143, 2149). The current Court appears to be moving toward the consistent application of the O'Connor endorsement approach and toward its de facto replacement of the tripartite *Lemon* test.

Another area in which O'Connor's concurring opinions have had an immediate impact on case outcomes is civil rights, particularly with respect to the issues of affirmative action and sex discrimination in employment. Both of these issues concern the interpretation of Title VII of the Civil Rights Act. The process of collegial statutory construction, like that of constitutional interpretation,[18] clearly affords potential strategic opportunities to a concurror. This investigation of O'Connor confirms this, as her concurring position in several cases was both determinative of the result as well as an overtly conciliatory overture directed toward coalition mobilization.

For example, in the 1986 affirmative action case of *Wygant v. Jackson Board of Education* (476 U.S. 267, 1986), O'Connor's delayed circulation of a concurrence evinced a clearly accommodationist purpose. By the time she circulated her first draft, the Court was polarized into opposing factions over the level of scrutiny appropriate for judging racial preferences. O'Connor's concurring opinion emphasized the consensus that existed among the justices as to the use of strict scrutiny and the necessity of a legitimate remedial purpose in adjudging a policy of racial preference (draft of 15 April 1986, p. 2, Marshall Papers, box 386, folder 9). Her subsequent drafts stressed the presence of "certain core principles" over which there was no "intractable fragmentation" and devoted substantial attention to showing that the disparities between the Court's and the dissent's versions of strict scrutiny "[did] not preclude a fair measure of consensus" (draft of 14 May 1986, pp. 3–4, Marshall Papers, box 386, folder 9). Jurisprudential rapprochement aside, the importance of O'Connor's *Wygant* concurrence lay in the decisive fifth vote that she cast. Because of this, O'Connor's presentation of a compromise position (allegedly embedded in the Court's current disagreement), emphasizing the narrow tailoring of minority employment plans to their remedial purpose, was significant for future cases (see, e.g., *City of Richmond v. J.A. Crosen Corporation* (488 U.S. 469, 1989).

While the brethren have been slow to heed O'Connor's concurring call for compromise in *Wygant*, she continues to deploy the concurrence in a strategic fashion in civil rights cases. In the 1987 affirmative action case of *Johnson v. Transportation Agency* (480 U.S. 616, 1987), O'Connor attempted to use her concurring vote to leverage Brennan, writing for the Court, closer to the centrist position she had articulated in *Wygant* (O'Connor's memo of 2 December 1986, Marshall Papers, box 415, folder 9). Unlike *Wygant*, which concerned race-based employment preferences, *Johnson* concerned a gender-based preferential hiring plan. This distinction was not particularly salient to the Court's central debate, however, which concerned how to interpret prior precedents on the relationship between affirmative action plans and "manifest statistical imbalances" in certain job categories. In her communications to Brennan, O'Connor pushed for an emphasis on a plan's bona fide remedial purpose, tying this to a finding of employment discrimination against members of minority groups. Evidence of such discrimination, O'Connor continued, was not unrelated to the presence of statistical imbalances (between blacks and whites or men and women) in the work force, provided that the relevant percentage categories were compared (O'Connor memo of 2 December 1986, and opinion draft of 2 January 1987, p. 2, Marshall Papers, box 415, folder 9). O'Connor's outreach from the center was ultimately unsuccessful in *Johnson*; concerned about a defection from the left by Stevens (over the issue of voluntary affirmative action plans undertaken by employers), Brennan added language to his *Johnson* opinion that compelled O'Connor to concur in the judgment only (8 January 1987 draft of Brennan opinion, pp. 11–12, and O'Connor memo of 8 January 1987, Marshall Papers, box 415, folder 9).

O'Connor's use of the concurring strategy was successful, in a somewhat negative sense, in the 1989 sex discrimination case of *Price Waterhouse v. Hopkins* (490 U.S. 228, 1989). As in *Johnson*, in *Price Waterhouse* O'Connor used her concurring position to negotiate with the author of the Court's opinion—again, Brennan. Once again, she retained majority-side membership and attempted to leverage Brennan toward her centrist compromise on actionable gender stereotyping and discrimination in the workplace. Her memo to Brennan, following his circulation of his first opinion draft, indicates this intention: "if you are able to incorporate these suggestions, I will be pleased to join your opinion. If not, I will consider writing separately to outline the concerns I have expressed in this letter" (memo of 13 December 1988, p. 5, Marshall Papers, box 471, folder 4).

In the end, Brennan and O'Connor were unable to come together on the question of shifting the burden of proof in such employment discrimination claims. Because of this, O'Connor reduced her concurrence to the judgment alone and wrote a separate, clarificatory opinion (memo of O'Connor to Brennan, 5 January 1989, Marshall Papers, box 471, folder 4). Her defection weakened Brennan's opinion to a mere plurality judgment, thus strengthening the potential, long-term importance of her concurring argument; yet the number, length, and detail of the memos exchanged between Brennan and O'Connor over his *Price Waterhouse* opinion indicate that this was not O'Connor's desired objective. She instead lobbied Brennan to accommodate her doctrinal views, using the medium of written, reasoned argument; when he failed to sufficiently do so, she registered her position and reasons for disagreement through the official medium of the separate opinion (see her final memo of 10 January 1989, Marshall Papers, box 471, folder 4). Her concurrence in *Price Waterhouse* signaled neither ultimate victory nor complete defeat; instead, it is evidence of the complexity of the decisional environment in which collegial courts operate.

In the legal area of First Amendment associational rights, O'Connor's concurring opinions have been moderately influential in generating new constitutional governing principles. Her key doctrinal contribution to the area was a new approach for delineating the expressive rights of associations, an approach labeled the "associational purpose" test (Maveety 1989). According to this test, the scope of an association's free speech is determined by its organizational purpose:

if an organization's function is primarily expressive, then its speech-related activities merit broader constitutional protection than those of a more commercially oriented organization.

This approach had its origin in O'Connor's concurrence in the 1984 decision of *Roberts v. U.S. Jaycees*. The case concerned a state effort to compel the Jaycees organization to end its discriminatory, men-only membership policy; the organization argued that this regulation abrogated its First Amendment associational freedom. The Court upheld the state regulation through a balancing of competing-rights claims; O'Connor, however, argued separately that a better way to proceed was to distinguish the associational rights of expressive versus commercial purpose organizations (468 U.S. 609, 635–36). Her approach also commanded the Jaycees to integrate because, on balance, the antidiscrimination policy did not interfere with its essentially commercial purpose. Commentators on O'Connor's *Jaycees* test have argued that it is, first, more broadly protective of women's rights, in terms of their access to commercial associations (Note 1985b), and second, a dichotomy consistent with an enduring First Amendment distinction between political and nonpolitical expression (Heck and Arledge 1986). The associational purpose approach to associational speech rights has had some influence on the Court's doctrine of corporate free speech, and O'Connor has continued to reiterate its utility and application (*Massachusetts Citizens For Life v. Federal Election Commission*, 479 U.S. 238, 1986; *New York State Club Association v. New York City*, 487 U.S. 1, 1988; *Keller v. State Board of California*, 496 U.S. 1, 1990 [Rehnquist, C.J., unanimous decision]).

Finally, even in the area of federalism, an issue area in which O'Connor's membership in a majority coalition is fairly well established, she has used concurrence to signal her own refinements of her conservative colleagues' doctrine. This is most clear in the 1992 judicial federalism case of *Wright v. West*, in which O'Connor was one of six justices who concurred in the judgment of the Court. O'Connor's concurrence was aimed at dispelling the Court's overly expansive reading of the federalism interest implicit in federal-state court relations in the context of habeas corpus review. Prior precedents, she lectured to her colleague Justice Thomas, have not held that "federal courts must *presume the correctness* of state courts' legal conclusions on habeas" (112 S.Ct. 2482, 2497, 1992). O'Connor's *Wright* opinion is a classic example of a limiting, or error correction concurrence and is concerned solely with doctrinal standards, not with the result reached in the decision. It is interesting to note that O'Connor's opinion spoke for as many justices (three) as did Thomas's opinion for the Court.

In sum, O'Connor's concurring voice has been heard, though not uniformly heeded. Clearly, she has used the concurring opinion as a device for jurisprudential and behavioral accommodationism. At times the alternative positions she articulates in concurrence have served as the bases for the settlement of future cases and the establishment of new winning coalitions; moreover, this study finds no evidence that her concurring behavior has marginalized her on the Court or caused a breakdown of collegial norms of decision-making. O'Connor's capacity for judicial and ideological independence, exemplified by her use of the concurring strategy, arguably has instead augmented her influence among the justices. Her pragmatic centrism, which partakes of both jurisprudential adaptability and alliance flexibility, has made her pivotal to many of the Court's internal disputes. This is the source of her potential for doctrinal influence, if not leadership.

Conclusion: Judicial Accommodationism and Pragmatic Centrism

This and the previous chapter's analyses of O'Connor's juridical record unquestionably confirm Howard's (1968) aforementioned observation: the variables of strategy and style are as important to an understanding of judicial decision-making as the variable of ideology. Both the substance of O'Connor's jurisprudence and the nature of O'Connor's intra-Court influence are unintelligible without reference to her judicial accommodationism. Indeed, O'Connor's accommodationism functions as what Murphy called a "grand strategy"—a justice's overall plan for integrating and ordering particular influence tactics into a comprehensive scheme to direct his or her action. A grand strategy is useful for two reasons. First, it prevents a justice from "becoming so immersed in strategy and tactics for their own sakes that he loses sight of his objective, the accomplishment of a policy goal" (Murphy 1964, 202). Second, the formation of a grand strategy compels a justice to take an overview of his or her current political situation and to establish a basis for choosing between a direct or indirect approach to executing his or her strategic plan (Murphy 1964, 203). For Murphy, the indirect or incremental approach, which consists in less rapid, less open, and less obviously goal-oriented maneuvering, was the more promising influence strategy, "despite its disadvantages of slowness and *lack of doctrinal neatness*" (Murphy

1964, 203–4 [emphasis added]). While Murphy's study of judicial strategy predates O'Connor's tenure on the Supreme Court, his description of the indirect approach and the conditions for its success bear a striking similarity to O'Connor's judicial situation.[19]

There is ample evidence of the jurisprudential and behavioral qualities that make up O'Connor's accommodationist strategy. A fact-based, contextual conservatism and anti-bright-line approach to rule making characterize her doctrinal philosophy, which is seen most clearly in her abortion rights opinions. The propensity to join the winning coalition and to retain majority-side membership has kept O'Connor from being marginal to the Court's discussions of policy. Finally, her use of the oblique leadership tactic of the concurring opinion combines majoritarian alliance with independent influence. O'Connor's role in shaping the direction of church-state jurisprudence can be interpreted only as an instance of this "inside-outside" influence tactic. O'Connor has been sufficiently sympathetic with conservative policy outcomes to make her an honest ally of the Court's conservatives—an insider with respect to the dominant judicial coalition—yet her own attraction for compromise, balancing-of-interest approaches, and nonideological resolution of disputes frequently compels her to challenge majority reasoning, making her an outsider by virtue of her position as a moderate. Given this, it is not surprising that she has spoken most effectively in her concurring voice.

Like her legal reasoning, O'Connor's concurring influence is itself contextual, that is, it requires the continuance of a centrist-dominated Court or, at least, a somehow polarized complement of justices. For the legal questions where such coalitional arrangements exist, the concurring strategy offers a certain leadership potential, and in O'Connor's case, her influence has been enhanced by her capacity to shift alliances during periods when no ideological bloc clearly dominated the Court. (This situation appears to be continuing, with the replacement of White by the moderate-to-liberal Ginsburg, with the increasingly ideological marginalization of Thomas (Toobin 1993), and with the recent Clinton appointment of Stephen Breyer (see Segal et al. 1995, 820–21, on these appointments' contributions to the persistence of the moderate wing of the Court). In other words, her pragmatism, antipathy for "rigid and uncompromising rules" (*Employment Division v. Smith*, 494 U.S. 872, 891; 110 S.Ct. 1595, 1611 [1990] [O'Connor, J., concurring]), and preference for case-by-case development of doctrinal principles (Gelfand and Werhan 1990) accentuated the pivotal position she held because of the internal divisions of the late Burger and early Rehnquist Courts. O'Connor the jurist has been a quintessential balancer blessed by circumstance.

In this way, O'Connor's judicial accommodationism has had an impact on the intra-Court process of deriving and adopting decisional standards. Contextualized balancing, itself a conservative jurisprudential approach, combined with the issuance of concurring opinions as addenda to the Court's decisions, seems firmly ingrained among the contemporary Court's decision-making conventions. O'Connor's contribution to the establishment of these conventions, through her expression of the decisional tendencies of jurisprudential and behavioral accommodationism, is clear, yet O'Connor the jurist has also been instrumental in shaping the content of constitutional doctrine. Using the aforementioned decisional strategies (of fact-based reductionism, retention of majority-side membership, and utilization of concurrence), O'Connor has effected important changes in the case law in several key issue areas. The specifics of these contributions to doctrinal development are the subject of the chapters that follow.

Notes

1. Statistics in Table 4.1 are taken from "Leading Cases" in *Harvard Law Review*, 1982–1993.

2. There is some disagreement among judicial scholars as to the relative merit of aggregate pattern statistics versus more episodic and qualitative evidence from "important" cases. With respect to strategic fluidity and the substantive significance of its regularity, this researcher relies on the latter data source while recognizing its descriptive limitations.

With regard to the assignment effects of O'Connor's coalitional mutability, see Brennan's 20 November 1985 memo on the affirmative action case of *Wygant v. Jackson Board of Education* (Marshall Papers, box 387, folder 1).

With regard to the support effects of O'Connor's mutability, note O'Connor's revisiting of her position since conference in *Bandemer v. Davis* (478 U.S. 109, 1986), reducing White's opinion to a plurality judgment (Marshall Papers, box 386, folder 1, and box 385, folder 9).

3. Her signaling of conditional agreement as leverage to induce consensus-building compromises in opinion language was ultimately unsuccessful in *Johnson* but successful—at least in part—in *Gingles* (see the exchange of drafts, Marshall Papers, box 415, folder 9; box 382, folders 1 and 2, and box 381, folder 12).

4. As one recent study notes, there has been a steady increase from the Warren to the Burger to the current Rehnquist Court in the proportion of concurring opinions at the expense of dissenting opinions, although the fre-

quency of total separate opinions remains fairly stable across the three Courts. In interpreting this finding, the same study comments: "Is there something about judicial conservatives that causes them to haggle about the details of opinions that support conservatively decided outcomes?" (see Segal and Spaeth 1993, 282.) Obviously, there is more of concern to these conservatives than the mere occurrence of conservative decisions.

5. James L. Gibson observes that political scientists have made little headway in conceptualizing the basic nature of the continua involved in opinion writing. While judicial voting has traditionally been analyzed along a single, unidimensional continuum (for/against liberalism/conservatism), conflicts in cases are frequently multidimensional. See Gibson 1991, 261–62.

6. Some studies make much of the distinction between special and regular concurrences, with the former signaling much more independence—whether ideological, coalitional, doctrinal, or personal—than the latter. Following this, one study reports that for the Rehnquist Court 1986–1990 terms, O'Connor was among the top three filers of regular concurrences (4.9 percent of her entire opinion output) but was not among even the top five filers of special concurrences (5.8 percent of her entire opinion output). (The top performers in each category of concurrence were Powell, with regular concurrence as 5.8 percent of his total opinion output, and Scalia, with special concurrence as 11.4 percent of his total opinion output.) See Segal and Spaeth 1993, 278, table 7.6.

7. This researcher contests the assertion of Cook (1991), who argues that O'Connor's voice on the Burger Court, especially, was muted by the fact that she spoke in significant cases only in separate opinions and was not assigned the opinion of the Court in a single significant case between 1981 and 1986. "Therefore," Cook concludes, "her impact as a member of the Court can be reported more accurately by describing her voting pattern than in analyzing her opinions" (p. 240). This researcher strenuously disagrees with this assessment of O'Connor's juridical record and thinks that the analysis of the evidence here bears this out.

8. The data reported here were drawn from the U.S. Supreme Court Judicial Database (Phase I), 1953–1988 terms. See Bradley and Maveety, 1992a.

9. The database subdivides concurring opinion into two types, regular and special, according to whether the concurror also joins the opinion of the Court. Since the interest at present is the simple presence of a concurring opinion, the two types are merged.

10. The data reported are from the U.S. Supreme Court Judicial Database (Phase I), 1953–1988 terms. See Bradley and Maveety 1992a.

11. Statistics in table 2 are taken from "Leading Cases" in *Harvard Law Review*, 1982–1993.

12. This study contests the assumption of Segal and Spaeth (1993) that the influence of justices' separate opinions can be measured only in terms of

patterns of judicial interagreement. Because the "agreement" that they identify is solely that of contemporaneous opinion-joining behavior, they under-
specify the meaning and the measure of "influence." See Segal and Spaeth
1993, 279–81.

13. Segal and Spaeth could be partially right in their inference that concurring opinion writing changes the consensual dynamic. See Kornhauser and
Sager (1993, 49, n. 80) on the rise of an "issue-by-issue discourse" (and the
increasing issuance of opinions separated into numbered parts by issue) on the
contemporary Court.

14. Interpreted in this way, separate opinions are "costless signals" in the
doctrine-setting game of the judicial actors. See Cameron 1993, 48–49.

15. Winning coalitions (majorities of five or more justices) are not necessarily more solid alliances than minimum-winning ones, given that as a coalition
increases in size, the ideological "connectedness" of its members may simultaneously decrease, resulting in potential fissures (Grofman 1982; Rohde 1972).

16. See Stevens's opinion for the Court in *Wallace v. Jaffree*, 472 U.S. 38,
56, 1985; Marshall's opinion for the Court in *Witters v. Washington Department of Services for the Blind*, 474 U.S. 481, 489, 1985; Blackmun's plurality
opinion in *County of Allegheny v. ACLU*, 492 U.S. 573, 595–97, 1989; and
O'Connor's plurality opinion in *Westside Community Schools v. Mergens*, 110
S. Ct. 2356, 1990.

17. See *Wallace v. Jaffree*, 472 U.S. at 67; *Thornton v. Caldor*, 472 U.S.
703, 711, 1985; *Witters v. Washington Department of Services for the Blind*,
474 U.S. at 493; *Corporation of Presiding Bishops v. Amos*, 483 U.S. 327, 346,
1987; *Allegeny v. ACLU*, 492 U.S. at 623–26.

18. Some commentators posit that statutory construction involves a different decisional procedure and set of negotiations among the justices than does
constitutional interpretation. See Eskridge and Ferejohn 1992; Eskridge and
Frickey 1988; Ferejohn and Weingast 1992.

19. Murphy's discussion of the justice who best typified the indirect approach to executing a grand strategy—Associate Justice Stone—is worth
quoting at length:

> Stone . . . preferred to move slowly and circumspectly. When in the
> minority he would often suppress his real views and silently join the
> majority, saving his [separate opinions] for what he considered to be the
> most important constitutional cases . . . he developed the practice, when
> assigned the task of writing the opinion of the Court, of refraining from
> writing a new doctrine in bold, broad strokes—a doctrine which would
> probably be abruptly rejected and, if expressed at all, be relegated to a
> dissent. Instead he planted seeds of new concepts in the dicta of his
> writing. . . . Indirection became a habit, and even in later years when
> there was a liberal majority on the Court, Stone still preferred a gradual
> undercutting of old, erroneous rules to sudden change. His tactical goal
> was for lawyers, judges, and government officials to ask impatiently not

why the Justices had made new policy, but when they would do so (Murphy 1964, 203).

O'Connor's accommodationism bears a remarkable resemblance to the juridical behavior attributed by Murphy to Stone. Interestingly, it was under Stone's chief justiceship that separate opinion writing and the decline of consensual norms first dramatically increased. O'Connor, too, is accused of fragmenting judicial consensus; in her case (and, arguably, in Stone's as well) the use of jurisprudential accommodationism (sometimes in conjunction with a behavioral accommodationist tactic) to disturb an opinion coalition is both a judicial strategy and a jurisprudence.

Chapter Five

Religion, State, and Community

It has never been my understanding that a concurring opinion suggesting a clarification of our doctrine should take
precedence over an opinion joined . . . by the Court.

—Justice Anthony Kennedy
Allegheny v. ACLU (1990)

With these words, Associate Justice Anthony Kennedy encapsulated
both the novelty and the boldness of the juridical approach of his
colleague, Associate Justice Sandra O'Connor. The church-state area
is perhaps the clearest instance of O'Connor's uniquely creative influence on the Supreme Court. Her work in this issue area illustrates not
merely her jurisprudential and behavioral accommodationism, but also
her adroit use of the separate opinion to shape the development of
constitutional doctrine.

First Amendment church-state jurisprudence includes the interrelated problems of state establishment and free exercise of religion.[1]
Establishment concerns state aid to or preference for religion; free
exercise concerns state interference with religious practice. Conflicts
occur because of the fine lines between state neutrality and state
hostility, and state accommodation and state favoritism. Interpretation
of the proscriptions of the First Amendment has long been divided into
two competing camps: the "separationists" and the "nonpreferentialists" (Levy 1986; Swanson 1990, 188ff). Separationists opt for a
strict but benevolent neutrality between the state and religion, sometimes characterized as the "no aid, no hindrance" position. Nonpreferentialists, on the other hand, argue that the state may accommodate
and even aid religious institutions and practices as long as it does not
indulge in sectarian preference (O'Brien 1991, 640–41).

Ironically, nonpreferentialists, or state accommodationists, can be

quite *un*accommodating of certain free exercise claims against allegedly burdensome governmental regulations, arguing that as long as the
state has not directly prohibited religious exercise, it is under no
constitutional obligation to facilitate it. To some extent, such tension
between establishment and free exercise is endemic to the First
Amendment, and it is just one of the problems that has encumbered
church-state jurisprudence since the Burger Court era. An equally
troublesome issue has been how to conceptualize the "separation" of
church and state with respect to establishment clause claims. Strict
separation—the so-called "high wall"—would seem to be the most
uncomplicated way to handle this difficulty (Swanson 1990, 200–1), but
the separationist position has never comfortably dominated the
Court's jurisprudence, even during the Warren years; indeed, since the
early 1970s, some version of nonpreferential accommodationism has
held sway among the justices, but this has not meant agreement on
the Court. Establishment clause cases have instead been the most
consistently divisive rulings of both the Burger and Rehnquist Courts.

The Burger Court made the effort to resolve both these problems of
church-state jurisprudence. With respect to the tension between state
establishment and state protection of free exercise of religion, the
Burger Court reformulated the balancing test for adjudicating free
exercise claims in *Wisconsin v. Yoder* in 1971. The test was generous
to the religious point of view because it was truly accommodationist:
it considered the centrality of a religious practice to the religious
belief, as well as considering the compellingness of the governmental
regulation in question.[2] This approach avoided construing what might
be hostility as neutrality. As to how to conceptualize a state establishment of religion, the Burger Court offered the now infamous "*Lemon*
test" in the *Lemon v. Kurtzman* case of 1971. This tripartite test had
its origins in previous precedents and tests developed in a twenty-year
series of cases involving parochiaid.[3] The test established a three-
pronged analysis of governmental conduct regarding religious institutions: first, a state regulation must have a secular purpose; second, its
primary effect may neither advance nor inhibit religion; and, third, the
regulation must avoid excessive entanglement of governmental and
religious bodies (403 U.S. 602 at 612–13). Also a balancing approach,
the *Lemon* test was arguably a move toward permitting governmental
accommodation of religion (O'Brien 1991, 649–50). The test was supposed to offer a more systematic—if complex—method of balancing
secular and sectarian needs; but it failed to provide clear and unambig-
uous guidelines for application, and its imprecise standards occasioned

criticism from both separationist and nonpreferentialist members of the Court.[4]

O'Connor's impact on the development of the Court's church-state doctrine can be stated succinctly. First, she has resisted the supplanting of the *Yoder* approach to free exercise claims with an approach that more uncompromisingly favors governmental objectives of regulation.[5] Second, she has led the move to replace the *Lemon* test with a less formulaic "endorsement test." O'Connor's innovations in the church-state area also attempt to unify establishment and free exercise doctrines around a single jurisprudential principle: that no state action may "make abandonment of one's own religion or conformity to the religious beliefs of others the price of an equal place in the civil community."[6] In other words, neither state endorsement of religion nor state pressure on an individual to "disendorse" his/her religion (via indirect state endorsement) is permissible under the First Amendment, because both extract a "price of community membership" that is too burdensome to be fair.

O'Connor's church-state jurisprudence is an attempt to wrestle with a broader constitutional issue: majoritarian power versus minority rights. Many of O'Connor's judicial colleagues over the years can be comfortably characterized as either pure state majoritarians (Rehnquist and Scalia[7] provide the clearest examples) or libertarian individualists (Brennan, Marshall, and, over time, Blackmun), yet O'Connor, although she is a conservative, is certainly not a Borkian legal positivist, and her sensitivity to states' rights concerns prevents her from elevating the individual over the community. The community membership lens through which she views establishment and free exercise problems allows her to validate the community majority and its choices while being attentive to the exclusionary messages of governmental policies respecting religion; hence, endorsement and its correlative exclusion—the message of not belonging, of being outside the civil community—is the key to O'Connor's approach to the religious clauses of the First Amendment (Levy 1986, 150–51, 155–56), and, increasingly, it is an approach that has convinced a controlling coalition on the Supreme Court.

Analysis of O'Connor's contributions to doctrinal developments in the church-state area should proceed chronologically, beginning with her first objections to the *Lemon* test for establishment clause questions. The alternative approach she devised in the establishment context subsequently appears, in adapted form, in her opinions on free exercise. In many ways, her earliest establishment clause opinions

have thus been the foundation for her entire church-state jurisprudence, and although she remains most successful in shaping establishment doctrine, her contributions have directly influenced the Court's
debate about the scope of free exercise as well.

Obviously, to influence doctrinal development, a justice must eventually convince a coalition of the collegial decision makers of the
rightness or validity of his or her approach. Public release of the
Thurgood Marshall Papers (Weiser and Biskupic 1993) notwithstand-
ing, court observers really do not know much about the actual process
of interjudicial influence, yet surely, the process of intra-Court communication is more than an internecine flurry of memos. To matter for the
record, judicial statements of reasoning must be public and must be
reasoning in the language of legal argument. By filing an opinion, a
justice personally and explictly influences the Court's doctrinal dialogue, for that dialogue consists of the public pronouncements of the
justices on the bench. The very publicity of the appeal to colleagues
on the Court is what makes separate opinions more significant than
internally circulated drafts or memos. Separate opinions should therefore not be dismissed as failed efforts because they do not immediately
convince a coalition to join them. Judicial influence cannot be measured instantaneously, because the nature of the doctrinal dialogue
is evolutionary.

Having said this, it is difficult, then, to know that a given opinion by
a given justice has influenced the reasoning and voting of fellow
justices. Exchanges recorded in private papers are certainly an aid
here, but so are overt recognition and public citation of a colleague's
opinion as a precedental source. In the case of O'Connor's use of
separate opinions to reshape establishment clause doctrine, the latter
evidence of influence is present.

O'Connor began her service on the Court in 1981, but her dissatisfaction with the *Lemon* approach was not revealed until her concurrence in the 1984 decision of *Lynch v. Donnelly* (465 U.S. 668, 1984).
Lynch was the first case to uphold a municipal Christmastime nativity
display, as well as being the decision that inaugurated the judicial
practice euphemistically termed "reindeer counting."[8] A five-justice
majority held that despite the religious nature of the nativity scene, the
city had a permissibly secular purpose in displaying it because it was
part of a seasonal exhibit that included Santa Claus, reindeer and
sleigh, and Christmas trees (Levy 1986, 157). In *Lynch*, the three-
pronged *Lemon* test offered little more than a justificatory gloss that
rationalized the Court's decision—a point not lost on Justice O'Con-

nor. While agreeing with the outcome, her concurrence rejected the utility of the "primary-effect" and "entanglement" prongs of the *Lemon* test. She articulated an alternative method of determining whether a government's use of an object with religious meaning violated the establishment clause: whether the government action conveys a *message of endorsement* (or disapproval) of religion (465 U.S. 668, at 687). Religious symbols may be used by the state without the effect of endorsing a religion or religions; for O'Connor, the key was the context in which the symbol or object appears (465 U.S. 668, at 692).

As is revealed in the record of memos and draft opinions circulated in *Lynch*, O'Connor signaled early on in the deliberative process that she would join the majority's opinion but write her own concurrence as well (memo of 1 December 1983, Marshall Papers, box 343, folder 6). Despite this action, she was rather peripheral to much of the discussion during the drafting process, which centered on a dispute between the Court's opinion author Chief Justice Burger and principal dissenter Justice Brennan. At issue between them was whether the Court had already begun, before the *Lynch* case, to abandon the *Lemon* test in favor of a more contextual and historical analysis of church-state interaction. Burger and Brennan were also in dispute as to which context mattered for First Amendment purposes: was it the physical-spatial setting of the display or its cultural-seasonal setting? (see Burger draft of 27 February 1984, Marshall Papers, box 343, folder 5). Interestingly, the final draft of O'Connor's concurrence split the difference between them over the context question: she inserted the word "physical" in a sentence mentioning the crèche's display "in this particular . . . setting," while proceeding to discuss relevant cultural acknowledgments of religion (draft of 3 March 1984, Marshall Papers, box 343, folder 4).

O'Connor's actions in *Lynch* exemplify the traits previously identified as jurisprudential and behavioral accommodationism. First, O'Connor's endorsement approach is clearly consonant with the notion of contextual conservatism. Her approach retains as much of the previous precedent as possible by recalling the "secular-purpose" prong of *Lemon*, and yet her test simplifies the rigidity and complexity of the *Lemon* approach, while being explicitly contextually sensitive in its application. Second, she acts as a member of a minimal winning coalition; her agreement on the result is thus critical to the case outcome. Because of this, her criticism of the reasoning of the majority is potentially more important to the coalition members because of her power as an ally—a conditional one. Third, she uses the device of the concurring opinion to announce her doctrinal innovation. This strategy allows her to bracket the holding of the majority opinion as well as present her jurisprudential views in undiluted form, all without sacrificing her status as a member of the winning coalition.

Not long after the endorsement test's debut, one law review article was commenting that its usage would replace the increasingly fruitless judicial debate about whether the *Lemon* test erected a "high" or "low" wall of separation between church and state (Note 1987). This assessment proved to be accurate. Beginning in 1985, Court majorities and pluralities explicitly acknowledged and employed the endorsement test of the *Lynch* concurrence as a viable analytic formula.[9] For her part, O'Connor persistently discussed her test in successive concurrences since 1984,[10] providing important elaboration on it in her *Wallace v. Jaffree* opinion of 1985.

In *Jaffree* the Court overturned an Alabama law authorizing a moment of silence in public schools for meditation or voluntary prayer. While the Stevens majority paid cursory attention to the *Lemon* test, the very first draft of his opinion for the Court referenced O'Connor's endorsement approach from *Lynch* (draft of 29 January 1985, Marshall Papers, box 362, folder 2). Despite this concession, O'Connor concurred in the judgment in order to more directly question the usefulness of the *Lemon* test in the present instance; her argument was that the standard establishment clause analysis was unequipped to deal with the potential free exercise of religion problems also present in the case (O'Connor draft of 12 April 1985, pp. 16–17, Marshall Papers, box 362, folder 2). O'Connor contended that her endorsement test supplied needed analytic content to the *Lemon*-based inquiry by "requir[ing] courts to examine whether government's *purpose* is to endorse religion and whether the statute actually *conveys a message* of endorsement" (472 U.S. 38, at 69). The *Jaffree* version of her endorsement approach retained the purpose and effect prongs of *Lemon* while articulating why government action endorsing religion is impermissible: government is making adherence to religion relevant to a person's standing in or belonging to the political community (472 U.S. at 70). O'Connor's distinction between (1) impermissible endorsement and (2) governmental acknowledgment of religion consistent with free exercise expectations drew fire from Chief Justice Burger. In the final draft of his dissent in *Jaffree*, he criticized O'Connor's "hairsplitting" and "infinitesimal" distinctions (draft of 31 May 1985, p. 5, n. 3, Marshall Papers, box 362, folder 1)—an early indication that

O'Connor's fact-based, reductionist conservatism would distinguish her from other conservatives on the bench.

A high-water mark of both the Court's reliance on and O'Connor's reiteration of the endorsement principle came in the 1989 plurality ruling of *County of Allegheny v. American Civil Liberties Union* (492 U.S. 573 [1989]). In this second "crèche case," Blackmun's plurality opinion employed the contextual analysis of the endorsement test. The opinion invalidated the display of a nativity scene unaccompanied by secular seasonal symbols of celebration but upheld a combined display of the Hanukkah menorah, a Christmas tree, and a sign saluting liberty. Blackmun explicitly acknowledged his use of the analytic framework of O'Connor's *Lynch* concurrence, both by direct citation and reliance on its principle of nonexclusion and its reasoning of contextuality (draft of 30 May 1989, pp. 14–18, Marshall Papers, box 477, folder 3).

Unlike in the prior establishment case of *Lynch*, in which O'Connor had been rather peripheral to the opinion-drafting process, in *Allegheny* O'Connor was at the vortex of an intensive debate over doctrinal language. The exchange of memos and draft opinions included Blackmun, Brennan, Kennedy, and Stevens, as well as O'Connor (Marshall Papers, box 477, folders 1–3). *Allegheny* was also an instance in which O'Connor changed her position from her conference vote after reading Blackmun's first draft of the court's opinion (memos of 6 June 1989, Marshall Papers, box 477, folder 3). In the end, O'Connor filed a concurrence in part and in the judgment in *Allegheny* (492 U.S. at 623), providing the fifth vote to apply the context-based endorsement approach to adjudge the religious displays.

O'Connor's separate opinion not only offered correction to Blackmun's legal analysis, it also defended the endorsement test against the dissent's vituperative assault. Dissenting Justice Kennedy objected strenuously to both its "flawed fundamentals" and its unworkable notion of a "reasonable observer" assessing messages of exclusion (492 U.S. at 655, 676); moreover, the first draft of his dissent, which was quickly joined by Rehnquist, Scalia and White (draft of 16 June 1989, p. 14, and memos of 20–22 June 1989, Marshall Papers, box 477, folder 3), lamented the undeserved influence of the endorsement approach, given its diminished precedential value as the creation of a concurring opinion (492 U.S. at 641). For her part, O'Connor responded by challenging Kennedy's notion that coercive proselytizing[11], and not subtle favoritism, was the only actionable form of religious establishment (O'Connor's second draft opinion, p. 6, Marshall Papers, box 477, folder 3).

If vehement attack is indirect acknowledgment of a doctrine's influence and importance, O'Connor's endorsement test certainly qualifies; but a doctrine's acceptance can also be measured by the actions and statements of its judicial allies. In the Court's major establishment ruling of 1992, both Blackmun and Souter devoted separate opinions to praising the merits of the endorsement approach. While Kennedy's majority opinion in *Lee v. Weisman* of 1992 invalidated the use of a nonsectarian prayer in public school graduation ceremonies, it did so without reference to or reassessment of the *Lemon* test (112 S.Ct. 2649, 2655–56 [1992]). Both Blackmun and Souter argued in their concurrences that the "message of exclusion" principle provided the needed conceptual framework for the holding of the Court (112 S.Ct., at 2665 and 2671–72, 2676, respectively). Finally, in the 1993 case involving after-hours use of public school property to screen a religiously oriented film, "endorsement of religion" phrasing was used in White's majority opinion and Scalia's partial concurrence (*Lamb's Chapel v. Center Moriches Union Free School District*, 61 U.S.L.W. 4549, 4552 and 4554, respectively). This language continues to be unsettling to Justice Kennedy, who filed his own concurrence reiterating the objections of his *Allegheny* opinion (61 U.S.L.W. at 4553).

It is fair to say that O'Connor's endorsement test has found reliable support from the Court's center: Justices Blackmun, Stevens, and Souter. Indeed, Souter—who frequently acts as a member of the Rehnquist Court's powerful centrist-conservative coalition—went so far as to claim that "this principle against favoritism and endorsement has become the *foundation* of establishment clause jurisprudence, ensuring that religious belief is irrelevant to every citizen's standing in the political community" (*Lee v. Weisman*, 112 S.Ct. at 2676 [emphasis added]). Unfortunately, official adoption of the endorsement approach seems tied to explicit "interment" of the *Lemon* test. (The language is Justice White's, from his majority opinion in *Lee v. Weisman*, 112 S.Ct. at 2678.) While many members of the Court voice their dissatisfaction with *Lemon*, though, the justices seem reluctant to overrule it altogether. Court opinions nevertheless continue to evoke the endorsement principle, furthering if not confirming its authoritativeness.

O'Connor's idiosyncratic but successful sponsorship of the endorsement test attests to a particular kind of quiet doctrinal leadership. Her assertion of a new approach to establishment clause problems has been subdued, both in method (the concurring opinion) and content (reconciling her test with the *Lemon* inquiry). Her success has also been somewhat subdued: no majority has repudiated *Lemon* and embraced the endorsement test in its stead. O'Connor has nevertheless been the agent of creative compromise for a fragile but controlling coalition in this area of church-state jurisprudence.

O'Connor's role in influencing free exercise doctrine is more complex. She has served as a bridge between the Court's nonpreferentialist conservatives, who are unwilling to extend special consideration to minority religions, and the Court's civil libertarian wing, which views both direct and indirect burdens on religious exercise as unconstitutional. O'Connor has used the vehicle of writing separate opinions to express support for a "least restrictive means" analysis of alleged governmental interference with religious exercise. One of her own majority opinions, however, seemed to belie this support and became a powerful precedent for the nonpreferentialist opposition.

The first glimpses of O'Connor's divergence from the majority on free exercise questions came in two cases in 1986 (*Goldman v. Weinberger*, 475 U.S. 503, 1986; *Bowen v. Roy*, 476 U.S. 693, 1986). In two separate opinions, O'Connor expressed her dissatisfaction with the Court's emerging tendency to dismiss free exercise claims without clearly articulating a standard of analysis. She argued that the Court should reaffirm its commitment to the long-settled principle that government regulation affecting religious practice must serve a compelling objective and constitute the least intrusive means of accomplishing that objective (475 U.S. at 530 [dissenting from the denial of free exercise claim]; 476 U.S. at 727–28 [concurring with the dismissal of free exercise claim]). In her concurrence in the second case of *Bowen v. Roy*, she stated that what was at stake in free exercise violations was government's denying a person an equal share of the rights, benefits and privileges enjoyed by other citizens (476 U.S. at 728). This statement hints at the "message of exclusion" principle that O'Connor had articulated in the 1985 establishment clause case of *Wallace v. Jaffree* (472 U.S. at 38, 67 [O'Connor, J., concurring]). In *Roy*, her approach nevertheless led her to agree with the majority's denial of a free exercise objection to the government's use of social security numbers.

Although O'Connor perceived no "message of exclusion" or endorsement of irreligion in *Roy*, her opinion did require and identify a compelling state interest to justify the regulation at issue. This concern would be absent from her opinion for the Court in the 1988 case of *Lyng v. Northwest Indian Cemetery Protective Association*. The case concerned the construction of a U.S. Forest Service road through national forest lands traditionally used for spiritual activities by American Indian tribes. Speaking for a majority of conservatives, O'Connor articulated a "coercion test" for free exercise violations: governmental action could not coerce individuals into violating their religious beliefs, nor could governmental action penalize religious activity by denying an individual an equal share of benefits of citizenship (485 U.S. 439, at 449). O'Connor's *Lyng* opinion echoed some the language of her *Roy* opinion but not its compelling state interest analysis. She argued instead that no compelling justification was needed for otherwise lawful governmental programs with no coercive tendencies and only "incidental effects" making it more difficult to practice certain religions (485 U.S. at 450).

However one feels about the result in *Lyng*, O'Connor's effort to distinguish indirect from incidental burdens on religious exercise is problematic because the distinction between them is not sufficiently clear to legitimately trigger compelling state interest analysis. As O'Connor's post-*Lyng* behavior demonstrates, her majority holding was less an opinion shift than a muddled exercise in hairsplitting. This leads to speculation as to how to interpret her action in *Lyng*. The record of memos circulated from the Marshall Papers is of little help here, except to reveal that O'Connor, along with Rehnquist and Powell, originally dissented from denial of certiorari in *Lyng* in April 1987. Their reasoning, as expressed by Rehnquist, was that the First Amendment question in the case had been improperly reached by the circuit court and should be vacated by the High Court.[12] In the end, however, O'Connor's dissatisfaction with the lower court's ruling went beyond jurisdictional quibbling.

Arguably, O'Connor's *Lyng* opinion exemplified the decisional traits identified as jurisprudential and behavioral accommodationism. First, *Lyng* was an intensely contextualized and fact-specific argument, a method of reasoning by exception from the general principles of free exercise doctrine. The opinion's jurisprudential conservatism is seen in the effort to distinguish the holding because of the case facts while fitting the case into a series of precedents. Second, O'Connor commanded a slim majority in *Lyng* (as Kennedy did not participate in the case); her linguistic manueverings could reflect her behavioral accommodationism, her propensity to be critical to a minimum winning coalition. Her doctrinal concessions[13] guaranteed an opinion for the Court, with her speaking for the winning side. Unfortunately, *Lyng* was a case in which O'Connor's judicial accommodationism produced a doctrinal lurch that was not consensus building in the long run.

Lyng's ambiguities became apparent in the Court's subsequent free exercise rulings, which relied on *Lyng* to jettison the compelling-purpose approach completely. The 1990 case of *Employment Division v. Smith* also concerned state interference with the practice of Native American religion—specifically, termination and denial of unemployment benefits to persons engaging in religiously inspired but criminally prohibited peyote use. Relying heavily on *Lyng*, the Scalia majority rejected the need for compellingness or least restrictive means analyses in upholding the state's actions (494 U.S. 872, 886; 110 S.Ct. 1595, at 1602–4). Further, in a bold assertion of its position on free exercise balancing of interests, the majority commented that the "disfavoring of minority religions is an unavoidable consequence" of a majoritarian system of government (494 U.S. at 902; 110 S.Ct. at 1606). The "insouciant tone" of Scalia's opinion—not to mention the result he reached—have occasioned much criticism (see Levinson 1994, 2), yet one such critic saved his most vigorous condemnation for O'Connor's action in the case, charging that her evocation of compelling state interest analysis did not include "least means" scrutiny of the religiously intrusive governmental regulations (Levinson 1994, 5, 10–11). As in *Lyng*, but for different reasons, this same critic would probably claim, her line drawing in *Smith* potentially causes more confusion than it dispels.

O'Connor filed a concurring opinion in *Smith* agreeing with the judgment only. Her reasoning was a return to her position in *Roy*: she reiterated that both directly and indirectly imposed burdens on religion were suspect and required a compelling state justification (494 U.S. at 894; 110 S.Ct. at 1610). O'Connor chastised the majority for departing from settled First Amendment precedent—somewhat unfairly, given the confusion inspired by her own *Lyng* ruling. She also repeated the concern that animated many of her previous free exercise and establishment opinions: that government regulation not make abandonment of one's religion the price of an equal place in the community of citizens (494 U.S. at 897).[14] In keeping also with her own anti-bright-line tendencies, her very first draft opinion objected to Scalia's derivation of "a single categorical rule" from the long and presumably complex history of free exercise precedents (draft of 9 February 1990, Marshall Papers, box 500, folder 8). In spite of this, she went along with the Court's judgment, deferring to the Oregon legislature's judgment that due deliberation of all issues raised by the statute's enforcement had occurred.

O'Connor's approach to free exercise continued to command attention in the celebrated "Santeria Chicken Sacrifice" case of 1993. While all nine justices agreed that the Hialeah, Florida, city ordinance banning the ritual sacrifice of animals was unconstitutional, they split over how to apply free exercise doctrine. Kennedy's majority opinion, which was joined in full by only one other justice, adhered to the principle that neutral laws of general applicability need no compelling justification, even if they incidentally burden religion. This seemed to be a direct repudiation of O'Connor's observation in a final draft of her *Smith* concurrence that even neutral laws can coerce a person to violate religious duties (draft of 10 April 1990, p. 11, Marshall Papers, box 500, folder 7). In the Hialeah case, however, Kennedy found no need to reach this question, because the ordinance's specificity violated the principle of neutral, general applicability (*Church of Lukumi Babalu Aye, Inc. v. City of Hialeah*, 113 S.Ct. 2217, 1993). Both the separate opinions of Blackmun (which O'Connor joined) and Souter questioned the validity of the "*Smith* rule" and reiterated the need for a compelling-interest showing and least-means testing for all laws with incidental or disproportionate burdens on a religion or religions. ("Incidental burdens" is Blackmun's language; "disproportionate burdens" is Souter's.) Souter, in particular, cited O'Connor's concurrence in *Smith* for its carefully detailed analysis of "substantive neutrality" toward religion (113 S.Ct. at 2240).

The call to reexamine the Court's doctrinal turn in *Smith* has yet to command the support of a judicial majority. Congress, however, offered a statutory correction to the decision with the Religious Freedom Restoration Act in November 1993 (42 U.S.C. sec. 2000bb), which in effect overrules *Smith* (Levinson 1994, 3). As a result of this development, O'Connor's *Smith* concurrence could likely be the basis of a reformulation of free exercise doctrine. Was O'Connor a catalyst? This is, of course, ironic, given that O'Connor's own fence straddling in *Lyng* laid the groundwork for *Smith*; nevertheless, as in the establishment area, in the free exercise area O'Connor has deployed the concurring-opinion device to articulate an alternative doctrinal analysis. Significantly, her concurrences in both areas reference a principle that would unify church-state jurisprudence: that state action "conveying a message of endorsement (or disapproval) of religion" is an impermissible "message of exclusion." True, the principle is somewhat vague in terms of the standards for its operationalization, yet the opinions that evoke it could be described as "a body of decisions meant to keep the peace between strong contending factions"—separationists versus nonpreferentialists, both on and off the Court.[15] Although she seldom speaks for Court majorities, O'Connor's jurisprudential views have remained at the center of the Court's debate over church-state issues. It is thus fair to say that she has been the most influential jurist in this area over the past ten years. As a judicial accommodationist and a true First Amendment accommodationist, then, O'Connor makes an important mark on the contemporary Court. While the lack of support from like-minded judicial colleagues has compromised the successful, formal adoption of her doctrinal innovations, judicial personnel conditions are never permanent. New appointments and the fluidity of judicial choice (Howard 1968) ensure this. Given this, the most unconventional of O'Connor's methods of influence—the strategic use of concurring opinions—may prove to be the most indelible.

Notes

1. The relevant passage of the First Amendment provides that "Congress shall make no law respecting an establishment of religion, or prohibiting the free exercise thereof." Since the incorporation of the establishment and free exercise clauses of the amendment, states too have been bound by these proscriptions. On the incorporation of this part of the Bill of Rights against the states, see *Everson v. Board of Education*, 330 U.S. 1 (1947), and *Cantwell v. Connecticut*, 310 U.S. 296 (1940).

2. The *Yoder* approach had conceptual antecedents reaching back to the early Warren Court years. An important precedent upholding the "least restrictive means" analysis for governmental regulation that interfered with religious conduct was *Sherbert v. Verner*, 374 U.S. 398, 1963. *Sherbert* held that a state must show a compelling interest to justify a regulation with even an indirect effect of impeding religious observance.

3. "Parochiaid" refers to state involvement with religiously affiliated schools or educational programs; thus, the church-state nexus occurs in the educational context and the legal question is whether state aid benefits or institutionalizes religion. Beginning with the ruling in *Everson v. Board of Education* (330 U.S. 1, 1947), the Court announced a "child benefit" theory that allows governmental aid for instructional purposes as long as only indirect assistance to religion occurred (see, e.g., *Zorach v. Clauson*, 343 U.S. 306, 1952; *Walz v. Tax Com'n of the City of New York*, 397 U.S. 664, 1970), but the Court would permit neither direct financial aid to parochial schools nor religious indoctrination or devotion in the public school setting (*McCollum v.*

Board of Education, 333 U.S. 203, 1948; *Abington School District v. Schempp*, 374 U.S. 203, 1968).

4. See, for example, White's concurrence in *Roemer v. Maryland Board of Public Works*, 426 U.S. 736, 768–69 (1976), Stevens's dissent in *Committee for Public Education and Religious Liberty v. Regan*, 444 U.S. 646, 671 (1980), and Rehnquist's dissent in *Wallace v. Jaffree*, 472 U.S. 38, 108–13 (1985).

5. Her definitive statement to this effect occurred in her concurring opinion in *Employment Division v. Smith* (494 U.S. 872, 1990), discussed below; moreover, Congress later seconded her position by passing legislation (the Religious Freedom Restoration Act of 1993) that in effect overrules the *Smith* precedent. Such judicial-legislative interplay resembles Ferejohn and Weingast's (1992) "legislative policy making game."

6. *Employment Division v. Smith*, 494 U.S. 872, 897; 110 S.Ct. 1595, 1606, 1990 (denying free exercise claim; O'Connor, J., concurring in judgment). For similar reasoning expressed in the establishment context, see *Wallace v. Jaffree*, 472 U.S. 38; 105 S.Ct. 2479, 2497 (1985) (invalidating Alabama moment of silence law; O'Connor, J., concurring in judgment).

7. Majoritarian populism is arguably the principle that animates Rehnquist's jurisprudential deference to laws that result from the popular will. See Maveety 1987, and Davis 1989. The political vision of Scalia is also one emphasizing representative leadership and judicial deference to the wisdom of popular political bodies. See Brisbin 1989 and 1990.

8. Or the "reindeer rule," as it was identified by journalist Michael McGough in 1990. See McGough 1990.

9. See Stevens's opinion for the Court in *Wallace v. Jaffree*, 472 U.S. 38, 56 (1985); Marshall's opinion for the Court in *Witters v. Washington Dept. of Services for the Blind*, 474 U.S. 481, 489 (1985); Brennan's opinion for the Court in *Edwards v. Aguillard*, 482 U.S. 578, 593 (1987); Blackmun's plurality opinion in *Allegheny v. American Civil Liberties Union*, 492 U.S. 573, 595–97 (1989); O'Connor's plurality opinion in *Westside Community Schools v. Mergens*, 110 S.Ct. 2356, 2359 (1990); and White's opinion for the Court in *Lamb's Chapel v. Center Moriches Union Free School District*, 113 S.Ct. 2141 (1993). See also the concurrences of Blackmun and Souter in *Lee v. Weisman*, 112 S. Ct. 2649, at 2665 and 2671–72 (respectively) (1992), whose supporting votes were critical to the 5–4 majority that invalidated the use of prayer as part of public school graduation ceremonies.

10. See *Wallace v. Jaffree*, 472 U.S. 38, 67 (1985); *Thornton v. Caldor*, 472 U.S. 703, 711 (1985); *Witters v. Washington Dept. of Services for the Blind*, 474 U.S. 481, 493 (1985); *Corporation of Presiding Bishops v. Amos*, 483 U.S. 327, 346 (1987); and *County of Allegheny v. ACLU*, 492 U.S. 573, 623–26 (1989).

11. This concept would resurface and prove important to the Court's debate over the scope of free exercise of religion, a debate that would again involve O'Connor and Kennedy as doctrinal adversaries. See discussion below at 86 ff.

12. In the course of the conference over *cert*, Stevens sent a memo to Rehnquist indicating that he would provide the fourth vote to grant review to *Lyng*, but only in order to reach and address the constitutional question raised by the case. Stevens would subsequently vote to reverse, joining O'Connor's majority opinion (Marshall Papers, box 444, folder 1).

13. Whether they were, in fact, "concessions" is doubtful. Consultation of the Marshall Papers revealed that O'Connor's main dispute was with Brennan, the author of the *Lyng* dissent. Their disagreement turned on whether the form or the effect of a restraint on religious practice was determinative of a First Amendment violation. Both O'Connor and Brennan asserted that the other had misapplied the compulsion factor in *Yoder*. See Marshall Papers, box 444, folder 1.

14. Interestingly, the three *Smith* dissenters, Blackmun, Brennan, and Marshall, joined the constitutional analysis or reasoning of O'Connor's concurrence, while differing over the result. See memo of 12 March 1990, Marshall Papers, box 500, folder 8, and memos of 20 and 22 March 1990, Marshall Papers, box 500, folder 7.

15. The quoted language is from Philip Johnson (1984, 839–40), who defends the Court's lack of conceptual abstraction in the church-state area as an exercise in political compromise.

Chapter Six

Reproductive Rights and Burdens

A judge who does not with some regularity reach judgments that conflict with his private policy views is not confronting complicated constitutional questions with sufficient disinterestedness or intellectual rectitude.

> —Leonard Levy, *The Establishment Clause: Religion and the First Amendment*

Some of us as individuals find abortion offensive to our most basic principles of morality, but that cannot control our decision. Our obligation is to define the liberty of all, not to mandate our own moral code.

> —Joint opinion for the Court, *Planned Parenthood of Southeastern Pennsylvania v. Casey*

In many ways, O'Connor's juridical journey through the abortion litigation of the 1980s and early 1990s epitomizes the dilemmas of the judicial role. Her difficulties with the *Roe v. Wade* (410 U.S. 113, 1973) decision and her concern for the integrity of its precedent exemplify a personal and almost visceral confrontation with the obligation of judging. For some observers, O'Connor's performance in the abortion cases has earned her the "lawyer's seat" on the Supreme Court, "one generally held by a justice more moved by the facts of the case and existing law than by ideological agendas." (Ellman 1992/3)

To a degree applicable to no other justice, the constitutionality of state regulation of abortion has been **the** issue of Sandra O'Connor's judicial career. Beginning with her Senate confirmation hearings, during which O'Connor was vigorously questioned as to her state legislative voting record on abortion, and continuing throughout her tenure on the Supreme Court, reproductive rights issues have been central to

91

public and scholarly evaluation of her (Roberts 1991, 95; Wermiel 1991, 129).

There are two reasons for this. First, the issue of abortion was of major concern to President Ronald Reagan and his New Right coalition, as was the position of his judicial nominees on the decision of *Roe v. Wade*. As Reagan's first nominee to the Supreme Court, O'Connor was the subject of ardent political scrutiny. During her confirmation hearings, O'Connor was somewhat circumspect as to her views of both the precedent and the constitutional ramifications of the abortion issue (Abraham 1985; Epstein and Kobylka 1992, 235); thus, abortion rights have remained an important touchstone for measuring Justice O'Connor's fealty to the conservative right. Second, because of the intense public focus on the Court's abortion cases, it was the area in which O'Connor's role as a swing vote (Roberts 1991) and facilitator of doctrinal compromise was first noted (Note 1989). O'Connor's pivotal position in many abortion decisions drew attention to the accommodationist strategies that characterize her juridical presence generally.

Although O'Connor's first forays into the abortion field were dissents, she was able to combine strategic majoritarian alliance with an independent voice. Her abortion decisions illustrate a particularly fact-sensitive, contextual reasoning approach, as well as the repeated and almost incrementalist use of the separate opinion as a signaling device.[1] The reproductive rights issue area is also a clear instance of victory for O'Connor as a Court leader, both in terms of judicial doctrine and coalition formation.

At the time of O'Connor's appointment in 1981, *Roe v. Wade* had been the law of the land for almost eight years. Since the announcement of the 1973 decision, a Court-inspired political furor over the question of legalized abortion had spread across the country. Most commentators now credit the *Roe* decision with spurring the mobilization of the prolife movement, whose aggressive lobbying resulted in a spate of legislative restrictions on the availability of abortion (Epstein and Kobylka 1992, 207; Craig and O'Brien 1993, 43ff). A recent constitutional law casebook categorizes the restrictions as those requiring formal consent and those prohibiting government funding for abortion services (Epstein and Walker 1992, 305). It was the constitutionality of these restrictions—and their compatibility with the reproductive rights claim articulated in *Roe*—that has consumed the Court's attention for the last twenty years.

As is by now familiar to most American citizens, the 1973 decision of *Roe v. Wade* held that the constitutional right of personal privacy, "embodied" in the Fourteenth Amendment's due process clause, "encompassed" the decision to terminate a pregnancy (410 U.S. 113, 153); however, while the right to privacy was itself "fundamental," the right of reproductive choice was not "unqualified" (410 U.S. at 154–55). In order to effect a balance between the privacy right and the state's "important and legitimate" interests in protecting fetal life and maternal health, Blackmun's majority opinion enunciated a trimester framework to guide state regulatory action. During the first trimester of a pregnancy, the abortion decision and procedure would be a private matter left to a woman and her physician. During the period "subsequent to approximately the end of the first trimester," the state would be permitted to regulate the abortion procedure in the interest of protecting maternal health. The basis for this increased regulation of second trimester abortions was the "now-established medical fact" of the mortality rate for abortion versus normal childbirth. Finally, "the stage subsequent to viability" is the "compelling point," with respect to the state's important and legitimate interest in potential life. State regulation protective of postviability fetal life would include regulating, and even proscribing, abortion, except where necessary to preserve the life of the mother (410 U.S. at 162–63).

Based on the state of obstetric and neonatal medical technology in 1973, Blackmun's trimester framework was interpreted to mean that a state could not prohibit first or second trimester abortions, because the "compelling point of viability" coincided with the third trimester of pregnancy (410 U.S. at 163–64). As Blackmun put it, "state regulation protective of fetal life after viability has both logical and biological justifications" (410 U.S. at 163), yet by 1977, in addressing the question of public funding for abortion services—including first trimester abortions—the Court had retreated to the position that *Roe* "implies no limitation on the authority of the State to make a value judgment favoring childbirth over abortion" (*Maher v. Roe*, 432 U.S. 464, 473–74, 1977). As subsequent developments seemed to show, *Roe* left some doubt as to the degree to which state interests in maternal health and fetal life existed from the onset of pregnancy, independent of the viability question.

Despite these inclarities, at the time of O'Connor's appointment in 1981 the Court had taken the position that state efforts to impose spousal or parental consent restrictions on a woman's abortion decision were constitutionally impermissible (*Planned Parenthood v. Danforth*, 428 U.S. 52, 1976). O'Connor's first contribution to the debate over abortion rights would come in the 1983 case of *Akron v. Akron Center for Reproductive Health*, which revisited, among other matters, state-imposed consent provisions for women seeking abortions. O'Connor's opinion in *Akron* directly challenged the "compelling-ness" of the point of viability and staked out an independent doctrinal position on the states' ability to regulate the abortion decision, a position from which she has never strayed (Epstein and Kobylka 1992, 295–96).

Of course, what has changed is the constitutional status of O'Connor's position: although it was a dissent in 1983, by 1992 her approach commanded a plurality of the Court. The Court's opinion in *Planned Parenthood v. Casey* of 1992 embraced O'Connor's rejection of a bright-line method for adjudicating abortion disputes and accepted her interpretation of the *Roe* precedent. While a plurality judgment is hardly definitive adoption of new doctrine, as a jurist, O'Connor has clearly been vital to the forging of a position of relative compromise in the issue area of reproductive rights. Whether O'Connor's conversion of the moderate center of the Court to her view is durable awaits the test of time, but whatever the follow-up to *Casey*, O'Connor's legacy will be as the architect of the unduly-burdensome analysis of reproductive freedom.

The accommodationist tendencies that are found in O'Connor's work generally are well illustrated in her abortion opinions. O'Connor's initial effort in the 1983 *Akron* case was a clear instance of her jurisprudential accommodationism, because of both the derivation and the construction of her doctrinal standard. With regard to the more behavioral aspects of accommodationism, however, *Akron* is atypical, for her separate opinion was a dissent, not a concurrence. A careful reading of her opinion nevertheless reveals the independence of her stance and the distinctiveness of her conservative position.

O'Connor's *Akron* dissent was an objection to the six-member majority's invalidation of (1) informed consent and waiting-period restrictions on first or second trimester abortions, (2) parental consent restrictions on minors obtaining abortions, (3) a hospitalization requirement for second or third trimester abortions, and (4) a requirement of "humane and sanitary" disposal of fetal remains. According to Brennan's conference notes, O'Connor initially voted with the majority on the invalidity of the informed consent and fetal remains provisions of the Akron, Ohio, ordinance (Marshall Papers, box 315, folder 1), yet, just four days after Powell circulated his first draft of the opinion for the Court, O'Connor indicated by memo that her view differed and that she would be circulating something separate (memo of 7 March 1983, Marshall Papers, box 315, folder 1).

The first draft of O'Connor's dissenting opinion did not appear until 5 May. Her argument condemning the "unprincipled and unworkable" trimester framework for abortion rights[2] drew heavily on the Solicitor General's brief for the appellant. That brief urged the adoption of an "unduly burdensome" standard for state regulations of abortion: the state would simply have to identify a valid state objective that was rationally related to the regulation in question (Epstein and Kobylka 1992, 240–41). Both the Solicitor General's brief and O'Connor's opinion emphasized that the particular stage of pregnancy involved was irrelevant to the standard of review to be applied to the state regulation. In O'Connor's words, "the point at which state interests [in health and potential life] become compelling does not depend on the trimester of pregnancy; rather, these interests are present *throughout* pregnancy" (462 U.S. 416, 459 [emphasis in original]). O'Connor also emphasized that this understanding of the qualified nature of the abortion right was implicit in *Roe* itself; subsequent decisions had reaffirmed that the constitutional right "protects the woman from *unduly burdensome* interference with her freedom to decide whether to terminate her pregnancy" (462 U.S. at 461, citing *Maher*, 432 U.S. at 473–74 [emphasis added]; see also discussion at 453).

O'Connor's endorsement of the "unduly burdens" approach was directly related to her perception of the logical and technological inadequacies of the trimester framework "as a means of balancing the fundamental right and the compelling state interests indisputably implicated" (462 U.S. at 459). Technological advancements in the safety of later-stage abortions, combined with medical advances toward increasingly earlier fetal viability, place the *Roe* framework "on a collision course with itself," removing any reliance on a "bright line" separating permissible from impermissible regulation of abortion procedures (462 U.S. at 457–58; 455). Logically, then, the limited nature of the fundamental right in the abortion context, together with the recognized arbitrariness of the choice of viability as the point at which state interest in potential life becomes compelling, dictated a more flexible, balancing-of-interests method of scrutinizing allegedly burdensome state action. What O'Connor seemed to be suggesting (and suggesting that the *Akron* court itself was following) was a two-tiered analysis for state interference with reproductive rights. Her dissent proposed that even significant obstacles to abortion services can be justified by a reasonable regulation, as long as an undue burden is not imposed on the abortion decision. The undue-burden requirement "represents the required threshold inquiry that must be conducted before this Court can require a state to justify its legislative actions under the exacting 'compelling state interest' standard" (462 U.S. at 463).

In rejecting the idea that judges must defer to legislatures as to what is sufficiently burdensome, O'Connor parted company with the Solicitor General's version of the unduly-burdensome standard. "The unduly burdensome standard," she argued, "is appropriate *not* because it incorporates deference to legislative judgment at the threshold stage of analysis . . . in determining what constitutes an 'undue burden' " (462 U.S. at 465, n. 10). In spite of this distinction, her approach sanctioned the same conservative results urged by the government's brief: that the ordinance be upheld in its entirety.

Substantively, O'Connor's *Akron* opinion is an obvious manifestation of jurisprudential accommodationism. She explicitly eschews the bright-line reasoning of the fundamental right/trimester framework in favor of a contextual, fact-specific assessment of the inhibitions placed on abortion services by the state. The conservative inclination of her "unduly burdens" test is clear from opinion language such as this: "the state is not required to 'fine-tune' its abortion statutes so as to minimize the cost of abortions," and "that a state regulation may 'inhibit' abortions to some degree does not require that we find that the regulation is invalid" (462 U.S. at 473 and 464). The conservatism of O'Connor's approach lies not only in its overt appeal to compromise outcomes, but in its evolutionary origins as a legal doctrine. O'Connor made a concerted effort to show that the unduly-burdensome approach had been the subtext of the Court's previous abortion rulings, tracing its pedigree to Blackmun's majority opinion in *Bellotti v. Baird* in 1976 and Powell's majority opinion in *Maher v. Roe* in 1977. Her point was to demonstrate that the "unduly burdens" understanding had been the precedental rule from the beginning and that the Court had mistakenly derived an absolutist position and unqualified abortion right from the *Roe* decision. The rhetorical and persuasive import of this argument is obvious, irrespective of its empirical validity. O'Connor was attempting to draw a moderate conservative coalition around a revised understanding of *Roe*, with the existence of the precedent as the consensus point.

O'Connor reiterated many of her views in *Akron* in a second, major dissent in the 1985 case of *Thornburgh v. American College of Obstetricians* (476 U.S. 747, 1985). Speaking as part of a four-member minority to uphold Pennsylvania's informed-consent provisions and postviability abortion regulations, O'Connor repeated her dissatisfaction with *Roe*'s "outmoded trimester framework." She reprised her endorsement of the unduly-burdensome standard, insisting that it was "not newly minted" in her *Akron* dissent and commenting that it had been "distorted and misapplied" but nevertheless relied on by the *Akron* Court (476 U.S. at 828–29). A new emphasis in her *Thornburgh* dissent was her indictment of the Court's worsening ill-suitedness to "the expansive role it has claimed for itself in the series of cases that began with *Roe v. Wade*" (476 U.S. at 746–47). "I dispute," she concluded, "not only the wisdom but the legitimacy of the Court's attempt to discredit and pre-empt state abortion regulation regardless of the interests it serves and the impact it has" (476 U.S. at 829). This statement clearly shows that O'Connor's objection in *Thornburgh* was to the Court's perceived disregard for the contextual complexity of each abortion regulation controversy. In addition to criticizing an ill-advised reliance on bright-line reasoning, O'Connor also chastised the majority for violating canons of judicial and institutional integrity.

The record of conference memos in the *Thornburgh* case indicates that O'Connor's colleagues were as yet paying little heed to her formulation of the "unduly burdens" test and its implications (see Marshall Papers, box 382, folder 7); thus, it is fair to say that her separate dissents were as yet having little impact as intra-Court signaling devices, but her *Akron* dissent substantially informed the content of the Solicitor General's brief for the appellant state (Epstein and Kobylka 1992, 254). O'Connor's pivotal importance, and the potentially mobilizing quality of her legal arguments, was definitely being heeded outside the Court. Four years later, her influence in the issue area of abortion would finally be marked by her judicial colleagues as well.

With the benefit of hindsight, one can see that the 1989 case of *Webster v. Reproductive Health Services* (492 U.S. 490, 1989) was an important turning point, in terms of both O'Connor's pivotal position and her contribution to the substantive construction of reproductive rights jurisprudence. Her tie-breaking vote in the case was incontrovertible, amplifying the significance of the views she expressed in her separate concurrence. According to one study, the amicus curiae briefs on both sides of the *Webster* controversy, but especially those of the prochoice interest groups, were overtly pitched to O'Connor (Epstein and Kobylka 1992, 268–69). It is thus plausible to say that her pivotal role in formulating abortion rights doctrine was fully recognized and realized in *Webster*.

"O'Connor was the fulcrum balancing *Roe*'s future as precedent," assert the authors of one recent study of the Supreme Court (Epstein and Kobylka 1992, 283); indeed, O'Connor's vote was all that stood between *Roe* and its reconsideration by the Court. O'Connor was one of five justices voting to uphold the constitutionality of the Missouri restrictions on abortion services. These included a provision prohibiting the use of public employees and facilities in performing abortions not necessary to save the mother's life, a requirement for viability testing where fetal viability is possible in the judgment of the physician, and a statutory preamble stating that "the life of human beings begins at conception" and that "unborn children have protectable interests in life, health and well-being." An additional provision, prohibiting the use of public funds, employees, or facilities in counseling women about abortion was unanimously declared moot, largely at the insistence of O'Connor.[3]

O'Connor's interpretation of the restrictions reprised her oft-stated views that since the regulations did not unduly burden the choice to obtain an abortion, they were neither impermissible nor inconsistent with the *Roe* precedent (492 U.S. at 529–30). She thus demurred from supplying the fifth vote to revisit the *Roe* precedent, arguing that the ruling did not "provide a basis for reevaluating *Roe*" (492 U.S. at 522, 531). She did, however, declare—rather ominously—that

> when the constitutional invalidity of a State's abortion statute actually turns on the constitutional validity of *Roe v. Wade*, there will be time enough to reexamine *Roe*. And to do so carefully. (492 U.S. at 526)

As with many of the prolife, "model" legislative efforts brought to the Court in the 1980s, the Missouri abortion regulation at issue in *Webster* was multifaceted. The split on the Court was as multidimensional as the statute it considered.[4] In many ways, O'Connor was instrumental in producing this split, which resulted in a decisive victory for the forces of muddled compromise.[5]

Inconclusive compromises aside, the *Webster* case contained an interesting dramatic element: that of O'Connor's strategic voting during the opinion circulation stage. A clearer illustration of her behavioral accommodationism combined with the "heresthetic" use of a separate opinion could hardly be found.[6] The conference memos circulated during the opinion writing in *Webster* reveal that O'Connor threatened a partial defection from the Court's opinion authored by Chief Justice Rehnquist (draft of 22 June 1989, Marshall Papers, box 480, folder 6 [partial concurrence], and draft of 26 June 1989, Marshall Papers, box 480, folder 5 [partial dissent]). Her concern was the mootness of the statutory provision prohibiting public support for abortion counseling. Her first draft of her partial concurrence occasioned this response from Stevens:

> your opinion has convinced me . . . and I shall write a brief opinion either joining what you have written on that issue or at least subscribing to your reasoning. I also agree with your explanation of why your construction . . . avoids any necessity to reexamine *Roe*. (memo of 22 June 1989, Marshall Papers, box 480, folder 6)

Blackmun was also so inspired, observing in his memo to O'Connor that he agreed with her conclusion and thought that "it might be possible for you to obtain a Court as to the [mootness] issue and it would drop out of the case" (memo of 26 June 1989, Marshall Papers, box 480, folder 6).

O'Connor's separate opinion writing here was used to affirm her pivotal position in the resolution of the abortion issue, and her attraction of Brennan and Marshall (see memos of 26 June 1989, Marshall Papers, box 480, folder 6), in addition to Stevens and Blackmun, threatened to upset the *Webster* majority. Rehnquist conceded, adopting O'Connor's mootness position and softening the language of his opinion with regard to *Roe* (see note 2 below and Rehnquist's 27 June 1989 memo to the conference, Marshall Papers, box 480, folder 5; Baer 1989, cited in Epstein and Kobylka 1992, 283). Following Rehnquist's concession, O'Connor circulated a third draft, returning to her partial concurrence/concurrence in the judgment position, which included a key insertion at page five that there was no need for premature reconsideration of *Roe* at this point (draft of 28 June 1989, Marshall Papers, box 480, folder 4). By retaining majority-side membership, but by introducing the mootness question to strategically realign the justices, O'Connor was able to influence the content of the *Webster* plurality opinion.

O'Connor continued to be influential and, at times, pivotal in subsequent abortion cases in 1990 and 1991. In the 1990 decision of *Hodgson v. Minnesota*, invalidating a two-parent notice requirement for minors seeking abortions, O'Connor acted with the plurality but introduced additional fine-tuning of her own. Her reaching out to Stevens during the *Webster* case had not been in vain: his plurality opinion employed the language of "minimal burdens" to hold that a one-parent notification and forty-eight-hour waiting period requirement for minors seeking abortions was a constitutionally permissible advancement of legitimate state interests (*Hodgson v. Minnesota*, 497 U.S. 417, 458; 110 S.Ct. 2926, 2944–45, 1990); indeed, she joined parts of his opinion on the strength of her interpretation of it as endorsing the "unduly burdens" analysis. She found confirmation of this interpretation to lie in Stevens's statement that a "statute cannot be sustained if the *obstacles* it imposes are not reasonably related to legitimate state interests" (opinion of O'Connor, 497 U.S. at 458; 110 S.Ct. at 2950, citing Stevens's opinion for the Court at 422; 2937 [emphasis added]). She nevertheless differed with Stevens as to the constitutionality of two-parent notification with a judicial bypass provision; on this question, she sided with the conservative bloc of Rehnquist, White, Scalia, and Kennedy (497 U.S. at 459–60; 110 S.Ct. at 2950–51). *Hodgson* was thus an example of continuity in O'Connor's juridical approach. As previously, she continued to use the separate opinion—irrespective of the coalitional position of its emanation—as a device to signal to the median justices (whoever they might be) that her centrist option was the only possible consensus position for the Court.

In 1991 the Court decided the abortion-related case of *Rust v. Sullivan* (500 U.S. 173, 1991). A new appointee, Justice Souter, had replaced the staunch *Roe*-supporter Justice Brennan. The case concerned the direction of federal funds for family-planning services to facilities or institutions engaged in counseling activities advocating abortion as a method of family planning. In 1988 the secretary of Health and Human Services amended the federal funding provision to prohibit fund recipients from conducting abortion counseling, referral, or advocacy. Five justices of the Court, including Souter, upheld the amendment; O'Connor was among the four justices dissenting from the ruling. In a brief dissenting opinion reminiscent of O'Connor's earlier troubles with state restrictions on physicians' counseling of abortion patients (see *Akron* and *Webster*), O'Connor argued that "neither the language nor the history of [the statute] compels the Secretary's interpretation" and that "the interpretation raises serious First Amendment concerns" (500 U.S. at 224). She opted instead for a narrower, statutory ruling deferring to Congress on the intended meaning of the federal funding provision in question. While Souter's position in *Rust* was taken (incorrectly, as it turned out) as a harbinger of his future votes on abortion rights, O'Connor's position in *Rust* was perhaps more portentous.

The most important abortion decision to date has been that in the 1992 case of *Planned Parenthood of Southeastern Pennsylvania v. Casey* (112 S.Ct. 2791, 1992). Though the case concerned provisions virtually identical to those invalidated in *Thornburgh* in 1986, the circuit court upheld them, "emphasiz[ing] that *Webster* had substantially undercut support for a woman's 'fundamental right' to obtain an abortion." The circuit judge authoring the court's opinion commented that "in sum, O'Connor's undue burden standard is the law of the land" (Craig and O'Brien 1993, 330). True to his prediction, the *Casey* court adhered to the O'Connor standard to uphold all but the spousal notification provision for married women seeking abortions.

Casey was a noteworthy decision for several reasons. First, it exemplified the Court's continued polarization and fragmentation over the abortion rights issue—there was no decisional majority. Second, it occasioned the issuance of a rare, jointly written opinion—the plurality opinion signed by O'Connor, Kennedy and Souter. Third, the decision represented a victory for O'Connor the coalition builder, because her unduly-burdensome test, combined with the concern for institutional integrity and the principle of stare decisis, commanded the allegiance of two critical votes, those of moderate conservatives Kennedy and Souter. Finally, the anxiously awaited decision unambiguously reaffirmed the *Roe* precedent, while "represent[ing] the kind of *political compromise* within the Court that was destined neither to please activists on either side nor to lay the controversy to rest" (Craig and O'Brien 1993, 328 [emphasis added]). This was because the compromise was "contingent on how and how soon the composition of the bench changed" (Craig and O'Brien 1993, 347). With the retirement of White and his replacement by Clinton-appointee Ginsburg, plus the certainty of a second Democratic appointment to replace retiring *Roe*-author Blackmun, the compromise would seem to be secure, but one price of this compromise appears to be O'Connor's complete estrangement from the radical right wing of the Court, as the impassioned rhetoric of Rehnquist's and Scalia's dissenting opinions in *Casey* suggest.[7]

Because of the extensive news coverage of the *Casey* case, many of the details of the decision are fairly well known. The Court upheld several provisions of a Pennsylvania law regulating the availability of abortion—requirements for informed consent plus a twenty-four-hour waiting period for women seeking abortions, one-parent consent with

a judicial bypass for minors seeking abortions, and reporting procedures for abortion-providing facilities—and invalidated only the spousal consent requirement for married women seeking abortions. A bare
majority of the Court reaffirmed the decision in *Roe v. Wade*, although
only three justices supported the judgment of the Court in *Casey* in its
entirety. Much of the opinion of the Court, jointly written by O'Connor, Kennedy, and Souter, drew on O'Connor's *Thornburg* and *Webster* arguments, particularly in relying on the unduly-burdensome
standard to adjudge the constitutionality of the Pennsylvania abortion
regulations. In reaffirming *Roe* as a precedent, the opinion contained a
lengthy section discussing the rule of stare decisis; this section was
apparently the work of Justice Souter (Craig and O'Brien 1993, 339).

In spite of the opinion's joint production, it is fair to say that an
O'Connoresque approach marshaled the moderate conservatives in
preserving *Roe*'s "essential holding." This holding asserted "the right
of the woman to choose to have an abortion before viability and to
obtain it without undue interference from the state" (112 S.Ct. at 2804,
1992). The opinion clarified that *Roe* sought to protect a "dimension
of personal liberty" (112 S.Ct. at 2808) in the interest of securing
women's "ability to participate equally in the economic and social life
of the Nation" by "facilitat[ing] their ability to control their reproductive lives" (112 S.Ct. at 2809); however, the opinion continued, the
woman's liberty is not unlimited, and so *Roe*'s unnecessarily rigid
trimester framework cannot be considered part of the decision's central holding, as it "undervalues the state's interest in potential life, as
recognized in *Roe*" (112 S.Ct. at 2818).

O'Connor's jurisprudentially accommodationist mark on the *Casey*
plurality opinion is clear. The decision exemplifies contextual, reductionist conservatism in its reliance on facts, not formulas, in assessing
the permissibility of state regulation of abortion procedures. The
opinion rejected the trimester framework as an "elaborate, rigid con-
struct," embracing instead the undue-burden balancing standard,
which weighs the "substantial state interest in potential life throughout
pregnancy" with "the woman's right to make the ultimate decision"
whether to terminate her pregnancy prior to viability (112 S.Ct. at
2820–21). The fact-specific nature of the balancing inquiry is evident
in the opinion's distinction between "particular burdens"—burdens
that fall merely on a particular group—and "substantial obstacles"—
burdens that place impermissible barriers in the way of the abortion
decision (112 S.Ct. at 2825). The opinion is also reductionist, in the
sense that its conclusions reduce to the presence of particular sets

of facts—arguing, for example, that "no change in *Roe*'s factual underpinnings has left its central holding obsolete" (112 S.Ct. at 2812) and "no changes of fact have rendered viability more or less appropriate as the point at which the balance of interests tips" (112 S.Ct. at 2812).

With respect to the conservative implications of the jurisprudential approach of the *Casey* opinion, two observations are warranted. First, the opinion stresses its preservation of (1) precedent and law's stability, (2) individuals' settled expectations and "reliance interests," and (3) the Court's institutional integrity (112 S.Ct. at 2812; 2809; 2814–16). One recent analysis of the contemporary Court reads this aspect of *Casey* as indicative of the Rehnquist Court's "backward-looking substantive approaches to the Constitution," a perspective defined as judicial reliance on established positive law or case precedent in making adjudicative determinations (Allen 1992, 686, 692). Second, the ruling specifically authorizes states to regulate many aspects of abortion procedures and their availability by removing the Court from an improperly interventionist role.

In a sense, *Casey* represents the successful culmination of another aspect of O'Connor's judicial accommodationism: her reliance on separate opinion writing to generate doctrinal options and to exert jurisprudential leadership. The plurality's joint opinion in *Casey* endorsed the substance of O'Connor's views articulated in her *Akron, Thornburgh*, and *Webster* opinions. The collectively written nature of the *Casey* opinion is, moreover, an interesting instance of O'Connor's behaviorally accommodationist tendencies. The collegial effort represented by the *Casey* opinion suggests not only O'Connor's facility for strategic compromise, but also the considered nature of the emergent alliance among moderate conservatives O'Connor, Kennedy, and Souter. This alliance's commitment to the constitutional principle of "precedential force" (to borrow language from Chief Justice Rehnquist's dissent, 112 S.Ct. at 2860), indeed, reflects one major difference between the moderate and hard-line conservatives on the Rehnquist Court. Whereas the latter see legal decisions in terms of an ideological or jurisprudential agenda, the former see legal decisions as part of a contextually sensitive and incrementalist process of doctrine creation. As O'Connor and the others comment at the end of the *Casey* opinion, the constitutional "covenant" exists as a "coherent succession," whose full meaning can only be interpreted "in light of *all* of our precedents" (112 S.Ct. at 2833 [emphasis added]).

Judicial innovations, like much in life, are seldom permanent. The judicial parties in the *Casey* case themselves speculated as to the durability of the opinion's decisional compromise. O'Connor's undue-burdens doctrine is far from flawless, but it does represent a potentially workable compromise position. Political observers have proclaimed that the result reached in *Casey* reflects mainstream American public opinion: abortion should not be made illegal, but certain restrictions ought to apply (Craig and O'Brien 1993, 327). Some observers would no doubt comment that only a judge who is a former legislator could be the architect of such a compromise, yet the irony of O'Connor's doctrinal compromise is that its very legislative character prevents its final settlement of the legal disputes about the parameters of reproductive rights and burdens.

Notes

1. See Maveety (1994) on the use of this term in the judicial context. Opinion language and opinion filing can be signals to both future litigants as well as judicial colleagues as to the direction of future legal arguments or the direction of future doctrinal development. In either case, conditional, limited, or contextually specific agreement with the decision of the court is being signaled.

2. Draft of 5 May 1983, pp. 2–3, Marshall Papers, box 314, folder 12. She would subsequently soften this language, removing the word "unprincipled" in later drafts. See draft of 10 May 1983, p. 3, Marshall Papers, box 314, folder 12.

3. See Chief Justice Rehnquist's memo to the conference, which acknowledged that "the principal change in this recirculation is the addition of a shortened version of Sandra's analysis saying that a majority of the Court agrees with appellees that the controversy over [the section] is now moot" (memo of 27 June 1989, Marshall Papers, box 480, folder 5).

4. The *Webster* decision was reported as follows in the *U.S. Reports*:

Rehnquist, C.J., announced the judgment of the Court and the opinion for a unanimous Court with respect to Part II-C, the opinion of the Court with respect to Parts I, II-A, and II-B, in which White, O'Connor, Scalia, and Kennedy, JJ., joined, and an opinion with respect to Parts II-D and III, in which White and Kennedy, JJ., joined. O'Connor, J., *post* p. 522 and Scalia, J., *post* p. 532, filed opinions concurring in part and concurring in the judgment. Blackmun, J., filed an opinion concurring in part and dissenting in part, in which Brennan and Marshall, JJ., joined, *post* p. 537. Stevens, J., filed an opinion concurring in part and dissenting in part, *post* p. 560.

5. According to one former Supreme Court clerk, Scalia especially lambasted O'Connor for her "attempt to please everyone" opinion in *Webster*.

Some suggested she purposively wanted to assume the role of pivot in abortion cases; a few claimed that "Scalia's tongue-lashing," both in conference and in his separate *Webster* opinion, "repelled her 'enough to stay her moderate course' " (see Epstein and Kobylka 1992, 283; see also Reuben 1991).

6. This term refers to Riker's (1986) conception of the heresthetic manipulation of the dimensions of choice as a political strategy. The heresthetic strategist disturbs the existing decision coalition by introducing a new choice factor or variable, around which a new, more satisfactory (to the heresthetic strategist) decision coalition forms. See also the discussion in chapter 3 above, pp. 31ff.

7. Further evidence of this estrangement can be found in the Court's alignment in the 1993 decision of *Bray v. Alexandria Women's Health Clinic* (61 U.S.L.W. 4080, 1993). O'Connor, joining dissenters Blackmun and Stevens and partial dissenter Souter, filed a dissenting opinion that argued that federal courts did have the power under an 1871 civil rights law to enjoin antiabortion protestors from blockading abortion clinics. Intimating that the majority's opposition to abortion rights obscured its perception of the class-based animus involved in the blockading activities, O'Connor stressed that

> this case is not about abortion . . . rather, this case is about whether a private conspiracy to deprive members of a protected class of *legally protected interests* gives rise to a federal cause of action (61 U.S.L.W. at 4105)

Chapter Seven

Racial Communities and Communities of Interest

> . . . when members of a racial group *live together in one community*, a reapportionment plan that concentrates members of the group in one district and excludes them from others may reflect wholly legitimate purposes.
>
> —Justice Sandra Day O'Connor, majority opinion in *Shaw v. Reno*

> [If] there is no duty to attempt either to measure the recovery by the wrong or to distribute that recovery within the injured class in an even-handed way, our history will adequately support a legislative preference for almost any ethnic, religious or racial group *with the political strength* to negotiate "a piece of the action" for its members.
>
> —Justice Sandra Day O'Connor, majority opinion in *City of Richmond v. J.A. Croson*

Does racial identity constitute a community of interest for the purposes of group-based representation and remedial compensation? The constitutional answer to this judicially polarizing question has increasingly been found in the opinions of Justice Sandra O'Connor—and her answer is, increasingly, "no."

The nexus between racial identity, community of interest, and interest representation animates the debate over two contemporary civil rights policies: racial affirmative action and race-based electoral districting.[1] Each legal policy addresses a distinct problem: the first, racial discrimination in employment and entitlements, and the second, racial vote dilution.[2] What unites these two problems is that both produce harms with a group-oriented as well as a purely personal dimension. The harm suffered by the unsuccessful job applicant or disenfranchised voter thus results from his or her racial group identity and the discriminatory treatment afforded to members of that group. That discriminatory treatment, directed at individual group members, nevertheless induces status-based harms to the group as a whole. These status-based harms include reduced competitive opportunity, diminished economic power, and deprivation of collective political power. The shared possibility of suffering or having suffered such harms creates a potential community of interest based on racial group identity.

Whether this community of interest is *legally cognizable*, for the purposes of representative and/or compensatory policies, is the question with which the Supreme Court has wrestled in adjudging racial affirmative action and race-based redistricting. For both policies, some link between race and a community of interest is assumed. In addition, the impetus behind both policies is some (general or specific) remedial purpose. The goal of equitable representation for the group—with respect to economic opportunities or electoral competitiveness—is thus predicated upon an agenda of compensation for past, group-based inequities. This intertwining of representational and compensatory purposes problematizes the use of race-based classifications. As a result, the legal cognizability of a racial community of interest—its very representivity as a group interest in any given situation—often must rest on some compensatory justification.

Racial categories do not uniformly coincide with legally cognizable communities of interest. This has different implications for affirmative action and districting policies. With respect to racial affirmative action programs, the problem is the extent to which racial classifications should be or can be used to identify the wronged class members deserving of special consideration in employment or placement. With respect to electoral districting, the question is whether racially drawn districts should be or can be the corrective for conditions of systemic racial vote dilution. At issue is whether race-based considerations in districting are necessary or desirable to protect the political integrity of a racial community.

O'Connor is a justice who has challenged the presumed link between racial categories and community of interest representation. She opts instead for a "racial neutrality standard" (Slocum 1991, 106), which questions the idea of group rights or group claims on behalf of racial communities qua communities. She argues that the use of racial classifications, whether in an employment or an electoral context, "assures that race will always be relevant in American life" (*Croson*, 488 U.S. 469, 495 [1989]) and threatens to "balkanize us into competing racial factions" (*Shaw*, 113 S.Ct. 2816, 2832 [1993]). She nevertheless eschews the adoption of any bright-line rule to govern affirmative action or redistricting questions and occasionally demonstrates a true ambivalence regarding the legal cognizability of racial group interests (Blumrosen 1991, 53–54; Slocum 1991, 106).

In both a substantive and a coalitional sense, O'Connor's position in the racial equal protection area is potentially determinative.[3] In two leading opinions in 1989 (majority opinion, *City of Richmond v. J. A. Croson*) and 1990 (dissenting opinion, *Metro Broadcasting, Inc. v. FCC*), she spoke for the coalition of the Court,[4] which advocated the application of strict scrutiny to all racial classifications, including remedial ones.[5] Since O'Connor's authorship of the 1993 decision in the voting rights case of *Shaw v. Reno*, she has also emerged as the Court's leading voice on the constitutionality of race-based electoral districting. Like the color-blind standard she upholds for affirmative action claims, the standard of review she articulates for claims of racial gerrymandering limits the "benign" use of race-based classifications.[6]

As is true of the jurisprudence of affirmative action and electoral districting generally, O'Connor's substantive position on the theoretical and legal relationship between racial communities and community rights evolved from two distinct lines of cases,[7] yet despite the distinctiveness and separateness of the racial affirmative action and electoral districting lines of cases, O'Connor's opinions in these areas produce an integrated theory of the relationship between racial and community identity.[8] In sketching the parameters of politically and legally cognizable racial communities of interest, she employs the familiar tools of jurisprudential accommodationism; and, while she now articulates this theory on behalf of an emergent majority coalition, she began its development through a series of separate concurring opinions in affirmative action and redistricting cases throughout the 1980s. In addition, because of the unsettled nature of and shifting alliances in affirmative action and redistricting decisions, O'Connor exhibited pronounced coalitional fluidity in maintaining her majority-side membership. Her opinion writing and coalitional actions in these racial community-of-interest cases thus dramatically exemplify her behavioral accommodationism.

The integrated nature of O'Connor's theory of the legal cognizability of racial group interests is best revealed if the affirmative action and electoral districting cases are discussed together. O'Connor's race-related opinions can then be evaluated as interrelated, sequential steps toward her current position. The validity of this approach is enhanced by the fact that O'Connor herself draws on certain of her recent racial affirmative action opinions in constructing the argument against race-based districting in the 1993 case of *Shaw v. Reno*. In the affirmative action decision of *City of Richmond v. J. A. Croson* in 1989, she likewise speculates that, absent proper judicial scrutiny, "there is danger that a racial classification is merely . . . a form of racial politics" (488 U.S. 469, 510, 1989). As the analysis shows, her affirmative action and redistricting opinions fall into three evolutionary stages. Each stage has contributed to her effort to locate racial communities of interest within a more general theory of community identity and interest representation.[9]

As with her jurisprudential innovations and accommodations in the areas of religious liberty and reproductive freedom, O'Connor's jurisprudence of racial classification developed incrementally. The first stage in her articulation of a constitutional theory of racial communities of interest coincided with three opinions—all of them concurrences—issued in 1986. These opinions all wrestle with the conceptual problem of the representability of group interests. In different ways, the opinions all attempt to set the definitional parameters of legitimate racial group-based claims. The focal point of these opinions is thus the problematic nature of groups for constitutional adjudication.

Of the three cases decided in 1986, one was a racial affirmative action issue and two concerned matters of group-based electoral districting. Interestingly, internal conference memos reveal that O'Connor switched sides or shifted allegiance during the course of decision in all three cases. All three concurring opinions are thus important evidence of O'Connor's behavioral accommodationist strategy, combined with jurisprudentially accommodationist opinion language.

In the 1986 affirmative action case of *Wygant v. Jackson Board of Education* (476 U.S. 267, 1986), the essential question was which persons are the proper beneficiaries of remedial action: those *identified victims* of prior racial discrimination, or *members* of an historically disadvantaged racial *group*? Committed to the goal of increasing the percentage of minority school teachers but faced with fiscal cutbacks, the Jackson, Mississippi, school system fired nonminority teachers with greater seniority than the minority teachers who were retained. The nonminority teachers filed suit, claiming that the layoffs violated the equal protection clause because they were racially motivated.

While the Court agreed with the non-minority teachers' claim, no majority opinion was produced. The justices were seriously divided over the level of scrutiny to apply to the racial classification, the legitimacy of the remedial purpose of reversing societal discrimination, and the plan's tolerance of preference for individuals who were not proven victims of prior discrimination (Haggard 1990, 56–58).

O'Connor's accommodationist behavior in *Wygant* is more interesting than the substance of the views expressed in her separate concurrence; indeed, she provided no straightforward answer to the question of the appropriate beneficiaries of remedial race-based classifications (Haggard 1990, 58, n. 41). She did, however, do two things of note: first, she apparently switched her vote between conference and opinion assignment, changing what had been the dissenting position into a majority position (see memo of 20 November 1985, Marshall Papers, box 387, folder 1), and, second, she profusely cited her colleagues' opinions in a vain attempt to show the existence of a Court consensus on the affirmative action question. In the final draft of her partial concurring opinion, she inserted statements recognizing the Court's agreement as to "certain core principles" and asserting that the differences between the Powell plurality and the Marshall dissent "do not preclude a fair measure of consensus" (draft of 14 May 1986, pp. 3–4, Marshall Papers, box 386, folder 9). For O'Connor, this consensus consisted of a recognition that racial preferences in employment must serve a legitimate remedial purpose and must be narrowly tailored to serve that purpose (draft of 15 April 1986, pp. 2–3, 10, Marshall Papers, box 386, folder 9).

Wygant illustrated that O'Connor was capable of strategic voting in order to preclude majoritarian affirmation of an unnecessarily rigid jurisprudential position. Her concurrences in the two redistricting cases of 1986, *Bandemer v. Davis* (478 U.S. 109) and *Thornburgh v. Gingles* (478 U.S. 30), proved that she hoped to shape the substance of a future jurisprudence of racial group rights. The content of these opinions conforms to many of the qualities associated with O'Connor's jurisprudential accommodationism.

The *Bandemer* case concerned an equal protection challenge by Democratic voters to an allegedly dilutionary partisan gerrymandering of the electoral districts of Indiana. O'Connor's concurrence differed with the Court as to the justiciability of the claim; she felt it was a political question best left to the legislature (478 U.S. at 144). Although the case concerned a vote dilution charge by members of a political party, the White plurality opinion likened the issue to a racial gerrymandering question (478 U.S. 109, 113); indeed, much of the justiciability debate turned on this purported similarity. O'Connor objected to the Court's assumption of a "group right to an equal share of political power" (478 U.S. at 147) and thought the decision risked "confer[ing] greater rights on powerful political groups than on individuals" (478 U.S. at 155). A parallel concern seemed, however, to be the Court's inapposite, noncontextually sensitive analogy between racial and partisan gerrymandering. She explained her aversion to this "reflexive application of precedent"[10] by outlining the distinctiveness of the racial community of interest.

> . . . there is a direct and immediate relationship between the racial minority's group voting strength in a particular community and the individual rights of its members to vote and to participate in the political process. In these circumstances, the *stronger nexus between individual rights and group interests* . . . suffice to render racial gerrymandering claims justiciable.[11]

Despite this acknowledgment of the identity of interest extant within the racial community, in the case of *Thornburgh v. Gingles* O'Connor questioned the representivity of this interest. *Gingles* concerned the standards to be used to identify racially dilutionary electoral districting, according to section 2 of the Voting Rights Act. The Brennan opinion for the Court established a tripartite evidentiary test for determining when a districting scheme had sufficiently diminished racial minority electoral strength so as to constitute racial vote dilution.[12] Interestingly, the physicality of the community—the geographic contiguity of the minority group and the districting plan's disregard for it—was an important part of the *Gingles* test for representivity and its violation.

O'Connor was a key player in shaping the formulation of this test, although in the end, Brennan's opinion and her concurrence found no common ground on the definition of racially polarized voting that actually impairs minority voter choice (see O'Connor memo of 10 February 1986, Marshall Papers, box 382, folder 1). O'Connor's objections to Brennan's effort to "mandate a *single, universally applicable standard* for measuring undiluted minority voting strength" (fourth draft of O'Connor concurrence, 22 May 1986, p. 13, Marshall Papers, box 382, folder 2 [emphasis added]) attracted the support of key centrist justices White (memo of 19 February 1986, Marshall Papers, box 382, folder 1, and memo of 27 May 1986, Marshall Papers, box

382, folder 2) and Powell (memos of 11 February 1986 and 17 April 1986, Marshall Papers, box 382, folder 1). Brennan was forced to make several concessions and overt appeals to O'Connor (memos of 13 March and 15 April 1986, Marshall Papers, box 382, folder 1; fourth draft of opinion, 20 May 1986, pp. 46–53, Marshall Papers, box 382, folder 2; sixth draft of opinion, 30 May 1986, pp. 15–17, Marshall Papers, box 382, folder 2), which cost him some support from the liberal bloc and reduced his opinion to a partial plurality judgment (memos of Justices Marshall and Blackmun, 2 and 25 June 1986, Marshall Papers, box 381, folder 12).

O'Connor's opinion, which eventually became a concurrence in the judgment, itself gained three joiners—Chief Justice Burger, Justice Powell, and Justice Rehnquist. In her concurrence, O'Connor expressed her consternation over the Court's "creation of a right to a form of proportional representation in favor of all geographically and politically cohesive minority groups" (478 U.S. at 85). Her concern stemmed from the plurality's emphasis on a minority group's ability to elect the candidate of its choice as the "linchpin" of unimpaired voting strength (478 U.S. at 92). In a seeming retraction of her *Bandemer* statement on racial group interest representation, she noted that previous decisions "flatly rejected the proposition that any *group* with distinctive interests must be represented" (478 U.S. at 98).

O'Connor's main concern in *Gingles*—as in *Bandemer* and *Wygant*—was the Court's alleged elevation of group-rights' claims to the same constitutional status as individual-rights' claims. O'Connor's opinions challenged the legal cognizability and thus the representability of group claims, because she questioned the presumption of a reciprocal identity of interest between the group and any individual member. Despite this problem, in typical O'Connor fashion, she ended her *Gingles* opinion with an appeal to accommodation. "Compromise," she opined, "is essential to much if not most major federal legislation, and confidence that the federal courts will enforce such compromises is indispensable to their creation" (478 U.S. at 105).

On the specific policy implications of a judicial recognition of group claims, both O'Connor and her judicial colleagues were largely silent in 1986. This would not be the case in a series of affirmative action cases in the late 1980s. In all three cases, O'Connor spoke for the segment of the Court highly critical of "reverse discrimination" on the basis of race, twice in dissent and once for a majority. These three opinions represent the second stage in O'Connor's articulation of a constitutional theory of racial communities of interest. Her 1986 opinions had qualified the representivity of racial group interests by questioning the identity of interest between the group and its members. Her stage-two opinions answered the question of why no identity of interest could be presumed to exist. Her answer was the rejection of the concept of racial group-level harm. The specific policy implications of this position were clear: racial affirmative action programs that went beyond victim-specific remedial relief were patently unconstitutional.

The first O'Connor opinion to begin articulating this view was her dissent in the 1987 case of *U.S. v. Paradise* (480 U.S. 149, 1987). *Paradise* involved a court-imposed, race-based one-for-one promotional quota for the Alabama State Troopers Association in response to its persistent and obdurate history of discriminatory conduct against black troopers. As with several previous rulings on affirmative action, the Court was fractured into a plurality over the application of strict scrutiny to remedial racial classifications.[13]

O'Connor's position in *Paradise* was essentially that the court-ordered affirmative action plan was not sufficiently narrowly tailored to survive strict scrutiny analysis, because the court had failed to consider race-neutral, alternative forms of relief (480 U.S. at 196). Without exploring the efficacy of such alternatives, O'Connor argued that it was impossible to determine whether it was truly necessary to take race into account and mandate the use of a racial classification (480 U.S. at 199–200). Even conceding, then, that group-level harms might have taken place, O'Connor was unwilling to conclude that a group-level remedy—one specifically acknowledging that harm—was necessarily required.

The cognizability of group-based harm—and the possibility of judicial relief for it—was thus questioned in O'Connor's *Paradise* dissent. One commentator has observed that this "fastidious quibbling" over the permissibility of the promotional quota was largely because her

> refus[al] to reject the fundamental fallacy that granting benefits to some individuals on the basis of race can be justified as a remedy for injuries to different individuals. (Graglia 1988, 605, quoted in Haggard 1990, 65, n. 76)

While such judicial temerity may have characterized the O'Connor view in *Paradise*, it was utterly absent from her subsequent statements in 1989 and 1990.

The first of these, an O'Connor opinion for the Court in the 1989 case of *City of Richmond v. J. A. Croson Company* (488 U.S. 469,

1989), has been central to O'Connor's development of a coherent position on racial communities of interest. Her *Croson* decision was significant for its vigorous repudiation of cognizable, racial group-level harms, for its firm defense of strict scrunity of remedial race-based classifications, and for its eloquent endorsement of a "colorblind" and individuated theory of equal protection. *Croson*, moreover, was O'Connor's first clear statement "that Fourteenth Amendment rights attach to the *individual*, thus making membership in any particular group irrelevant to the quantum of an individual's right of equal treatment" (Haggard 1990, 73–74).

The *Croson* case concerned a municipal set-aside affirmative action program for minority contractors in Richmond's local construction industry. The city mandated a thirty-percent set-aside figure for public works contracts, arguing that the race-based measures were necessary to ameliorate the effects of past discrimination on employment opportunities for minority group members. A 6–3 majority of the Court agreed that the municipal ordinance violated the equal protection clause. O'Connor's opinion for the Court stated clearly that the thirty-percent "quota" was not narrowly tailored to any legitimate remedial purpose—indeed, it was narrowly tailored only to the goal of "outright racial balancing" (488 U.S. at 507). That the city's purpose was not to remedy past discrimination seemed evident on two counts: the "random inclusion" of racial minority groups within the thirty-percent set-aside who may never have suffered from discrimination (or even resided) in Richmond's economy (488 U.S. at 506) and, interestingly, the policy's tinge of racial politics as the product of a black majority city council (488 U.S. at 507).

O'Connor flatly rejected the argument that a statistical, racial imbalance in Richmond's construction industry was evidence of racial discrimination, maintaining that "identified discrimination . . . in particular cases" was the only appropriate object of remedial racial classifications (488 U.S. at 509). Her repudiation of Richmond's construction of group-based harm was directly tied to her insistence that remedial action must be directed at individuals. "To whatever racial group these citizens belong," O'Connor opined, *"their 'personal rights' to be treated with equal dignity and respect* are implicated by a rigid rule erecting race as the sole criterion in an aspect of public decision making" (488 U.S. at 493). Clearly, O'Connor's *Croson* opinion is the logical continuation of her *Wygant* and *Gingles* concurrences, in that *Croson* ties the constitutionally problematic nature of groups to the illimitability of group-based harm. "To accept

Richmond's claim that past societal discrimination alone can serve as the basis for rigid racial preferences," she argued, "would be to open the door to competing claims for 'remedial relief' for every disadvantaged group" (488 U.S. at 505).

One commentator has argued that *Croson* represents O'Connor's realization that "there was no form of racial affirmative action that the [then] liberal wing of the Court was unwilling to endorse, making her consensus by compromise approach [as in *Wygant*] a futile dream" and removing any "further reason to mask her true commitment to the principle of non-discrimination" (Haggard 1990, 50). This is a fair characterization of both the *Croson* decision and O'Connor's dissent in the 5–4 ruling in *Metro Broadcasting, Inc. v. FCC* (497 U.S. 547; 110 S.Ct. 2997, 1990). *Metro Broadcasting* also is interesting because it was an affirmative action case that both the Brennan majority and the O'Connor dissent likened to a racial vote dilution question. As such, it is an important transition opinion to O'Connor's major racial districting rulings of the 1990s.

Metro Broadcasting concerned the constitutionality of an FCC minority preference policy for granting licenses for new broadcast stations. The FCC policy, which Congress had endorsed in legislation, aimed to increase minority ownership in broadcasting and thus diversify broadcast programming. Brennan's opinion for the majority upheld the policy as a "benign race-conscious measure" that served "important governmental objectives" and was "substantially related to achievement of those objectives" (497 U.S. at 564; 110 S.Ct. at 3008–9). Brennan's justification for not applying strict scrutiny to the racial classification was that it was a policy mandated by Congress, which was entitled to a higher level of deference. He emphasized, moreover, the importance of the diversity objective, arguing that it, as well as many voting rights cases, "operate on the assumption that minorities have particular viewpoints and interests worthy of protection" and that a state may thus "deliberately creat[e] or preserv[e] black majorities in particular districts"—or radio stations (497 U.S. at 583; 110 S.Ct. at 3019).

O'Connor objected strenuously to this treatment of citizens "[not] as individuals, [but] as simply components of a racial, religious, sexual or national class" (497 U.S. at 602). That group members were regarded as utterly fungible was, for O'Connor, evidence that "*proportional representation* of various races" and "outright racial balancing"—through the equation of racial identity with distinct views and behavior—was the undisguised goal of the FCC policy (497 U.S.

625; 110 S.Ct. 3035 [emphasis added]). Her feeling that "benign racial classification is a contradiction in terms" (497 U.S. at 609) stemmed from her concern that a societal concept of racial group-level harm was illimitable. "Untethered to narrowly confined remedial notions," she warned, " 'benign' carries with it no independent meaning, but reflects only acceptance of the current generation's conclusion that a *politically acceptable burden*, imposed on particular citizens on the basis of race, is reasonable" (497 U.S. at 610 [emphasis added]). As in *Croson*, in *Metro Broadcasting* O'Connor questioned whether racial politics was being elevated over legal correctness.

Also like the *Croson* decision, O'Connor's *Metro Broadcasting* dissent reaffirmed the application of strict scrutiny to all race-based classifications. Because such scrutiny included a searching examination of the "compellingness" of the governmental objectives, and because the only legitimately compelling state interest is remedying prior discrimination (497 U.S. at 623; 110 S.Ct. 3034), the effect of her opinion was, again, an endorsement of "colorblind" equal protection jurisprudence. Specifically, the *Metro Broadcasting* dissent unequivocally rejects the legal cognizability of diffuse, group-level harm resulting from societal discrimination and calling for overinclusive race-based remedies (Haggard 1990, 84–85). In addition, because of its questioning of the goal of racially proportional representation, O'Connor's *Metro Broadcasting* opinion is an interesting link with the racial districting cases.[14] As such, it shows that the rejection of the concept of racial group-level harm is directly connected to the problem of the representability of racial group interests.

This latter concern leads to the central conclusion of O'Connor's stage-three opinions: the repudiation of the political representation of purely racial communities of interest. These opinions, which include a major decision in 1993 and two concurrences from 1994, propose a revision of voting rights law and related race-based districting policies by emphasizing the unstable physicality of the racial community. In other words, the opinions challenge the automatic equation of the racial group with a political community and, therefore, with a *districtable* community of interest.

In *Thornburgh v. Gingles* in 1986, the Brennan plurality had held that racial vote-dilution claims turned on a districting plan's disregard for the size and geographical compactness, as well as the political cohesiveness, of a minority voting bloc. In order to comply with the *Gingles* directive, states began to create "majority-minority," race-based districts. Practically, these districts often could not be terribly compact or contiguous; moreover, in order to incorporate a sufficient percentage of minority voters, the districts covered a broad territorial range and so violated certain nonracial, community of interest concerns in districting.[15]

Such majority-minority districting occurred in the 1990 reapportionment plan for North Carolina's congressional districts. This plan was challenged before the Supreme Court in the 1993 case of *Shaw v. Reno.* A group of North Carolina voters alleged that two majority-black districts concentrated a majority of black voters arbitrarily without regard to considerations such as compactness, contiguousness, geographical boundaries, or political subdivisions in order to create congressional districts along racial lines and ensure the election of two black representatives. The voters—who were white—claimed a violation of the equal protection clause, because the plan was an unjustifiable effort to segregate voters into separate districts on the basis of race, abridging their constitutional right to participate in a "colorblind" electoral process (113 S.Ct. 2816, 2824). Without ruling on the substance of the specific claim in *Shaw*, the five-judge majority left no doubt that such race-based districting was inherently suspect and would be adjudged according to strict scrutiny.

Speaking for the Court in *Shaw*, O'Connor formulated a provisional test for the constitutionality of "benign" or "remedial" racial gerrymanders. She observed that

> A reapportionment plan that includes in one district individuals who belong to the same race, but who are otherwise widely separated by geographic and political boundaries, and who may have little in common with one another but the color of their skin, bears an uncomfortable resemblance to political apartheid. (113 S. Ct. at 2827)

Because such racial separation threatens to undermine representative democracy "by signaling to elected officials that they represent a particular racial *group* rather than their constituency as a whole," it must satisfy a compelling state purpose (113 S.Ct. at 2827). In adducing whether a state's purpose is sufficiently compelling to survive close judicial scrutiny, O'Connor posited that race-based districting—even as a remedial response to racially polarized voting—is constitutionally permissible only when (1) the state employs "sound districting principles" and (2) the "racial group's residential patterns afford the opportunity of creating districts in which they will be in the majority."[16]

O'Connor's point of emphasis in *Shaw* was that unless a racial group constitutes an actual political and territorial community, it cannot be a districtable community of interest. Even so, a racially based districting scheme must survive strict judicial scrutiny, because "racial classifications of any sort pose the risk of lasting harm to our society."[17] Despite the seeming severity of O'Connor's view, the jurisprudential accommodationism of her position is apparent when compared with the more stringent formulations from her conservative colleagues in two voting-rights cases subsequent to *Shaw.*

In 1994 the Court decided two race and electoral representation cases that were, in some ways, follow-ups to *Shaw.* The first of these, *Holder v. Hall* (114 S.Ct. 2581, 1994), concerned the somewhat specialized problem of the racially dilutionary effect of Georgia's single-member commission form of county government. Black voters claimed that the size of the governing authority was maintained with the intent to minimize the political influence of black voters as a group, in violation of the Fourteenth Amendment and the Voting Rights Act. Kennedy's plurality opinion for the Court rejected the statutory claim, arguing that the size of a governing body is not subject to a vote dilution challenge under the Act, and remanded the constitutional claim for further consideration. O'Connor was a partial concurror, as were Thomas and Scalia. An interesting feature of the *Holder* decision was Thomas's strident and far-reaching concurring opinion, in which he suggested overruling *Gingles* as erroneously holding that section 2 covers districting systems and electoral practices that affect the "weight" given to a ballot duly cast (114 S.Ct. at 2593).

Arguably, O'Connor was the pivot to whom both the Kennedy and the Thomas factions appealed in their written opinions. Both the Kennedy opinion and the Thomas concurrence in the judgment made ample reference to her *Shaw* opinion, her *Gingles* concurrence, and her *Holder* concurrence (114 S.Ct. at 2583, 2591). Thomas, in particular, made several overt appeals to O'Connor by copiously citing her *Gingles* concurrence and *Shaw* decision, as well as specifically agreeing with her concern in *Bandemer* that expansive readings of potentially dilutive voting practices "would distort the focus on the individual, for a vote dilution claim necessarily depends on the assertion of a group right" (114 S.Ct. at 2598). O'Connor's comparatively brief concurrence emphasized a single point: given the discrepancies in size among state and local governing authorities, no reasonable and workable benchmark for the vote-dilution comparison exists (114 S.Ct. at 2588). She thus distanced herself from both the bright-line construction espoused by Kennedy and the brazen repudiation of precedent by

Thomas. In keeping with her own behavioral accommodationism, O'Connor attempted to find common ground between the Kennedy opinion and the Blackmun dissent, doing so, once again, from the position of majority-side membership.

The second case, of *Johnson v. DeGrandy* (114 S.Ct. 2647), was substantively more important for the question of the districtability of racial group interests. In *DeGrandy* the Court examined the question of whether a reapportionment plan diluted the voting strength of a group of minority voters by a "failure to maximize" the number of majority-minority districts and, thus, the proportional electoral strength of the minority group. In rejecting the section 2 claim, the Souter majority emphasized that vote dilution was not the same as the failure to guarantee minority voters maximum political influence, or, as Souter put it, "the failure to guarantee a political feast" (114 S.Ct. at 2660). Souter's majority opinion was particularly interesting for its specific reliance on O'Connor's contextual reading of the *Gingles* dilution criteria (114 S.Ct. at 2657), as well as for its generally anti-bright-line language (114 S.Ct. at 2661).

O'Connor's concurring contribution in *DeGrandy* was simply clarificatory, reflecting full agreement with the Souter majority's "carefully crafted approach" (114 S.Ct. at 2664). She agreed that racial vote dilution cannot be equated with failure to maximize the number of reasonably compact majority-minority districts and stated "the opinion's central teaching" as follows:

> Proportionality—defined as the relationship between the number of majority-minority voting districts and the minority group's share of the relevant population—is *always* relevant evidence in determining vote dilution, but is *never* itself dispositive. (114 S.Ct. at 2664)

Her *DeGrandy* concurrence reveals once again her contextual conservatism and anti-bright-line jurisprudence. "Lack of proportionality," she commented, "can never by itself prove dilution, for courts must always carefully and searchingly review the totality of the circumstances, including the extent to which minority groups have access to the political process" (114 S.Ct. at 2664); yet her concurrence also exhibits her maddening tendency to straddle the fence: "Nor does the presence of proportionality," she continued, "prove the absence of dilution. Proportionality . . . does not immunize [state] election schemes from section 2 challenge" (114 S.Ct. at 2664). While her concern in *DeGrandy* was obviously to forestall any recognition of group rights to proportional representation as the foundation of voting rights law, her position on the political salience of the racial community of interest was somewhat cryptic.

In conclusion, can it be said that O'Connor has a developed constitutional theory of racial communities of interest and interest representation? Clearly, she has made important doctrinal contributions in the racial affirmative action and electoral redistricting decisions. She rejects an expansive concept of racial group-level harm and thus a correlative community of interest based on race. She prefers to use race-based classifications circumspectly and certainly not as a vehicle for the proportional representation of racial groups qua groups. She remains firm, however, that the racial community is a legally cognizable and representable political community under certain circumstances.

In sum, her juridical position is one of interest accommodation, where the interests at stake are both those of her judicial colleagues and those on either side of the debate about remedial race-based classifications. Her attempt to appeal to the various interests on the Court has been well documented. In addition, she has attempted an accommodation between two distinct philosophies of racial identity and civil rights: colorblind individualism and group-conscious community empowerment. Unfortunately, O'Connor's accommodationist jurisprudence seems an all-too-accurate reflection of the contemporary irreconcilability of these two philosophies of racial equality.

Notes

1. Grofman (1993) argues that voting rights questions "lack most if not all of the attributes commonly attributed to affirmative action programs." Grofman nevertheless does acknowledge that "voting rights, like other Fourteenth Amendment concerns, has developed a view of 'group' rights and 'group' remedies" (Grofman 1993, 1244). It is this contemporary legal fixation on group identity and group-based claims—and the emphasis on racial groupings as the cohesive locus—that animates O'Connor's jurisprudential response. On the origin of a group-based approach to representation questions, see Maveety (1991b).

2. Vote dilution occurs when electoral district lines are manipulated (often referred to as gerrymandering) or at-large electoral systems are employed that reduce the political strength of a group of votes or voters. Vote dilution tactics have been associated with intentional racial vote abridgement, where the

diluted votes are those of a racial minority group (Maveety 1991b, 100–4; see also "Symposium" 1995).

3. For one commentator, this is "precisely because she has a thoughtful judicial style" (see Blumrosen 1991, 54). Another commentator identifies O'Connor as "the Supreme Court's prominent voice on the constitutionality of racial affirmative action programs" (Note 1991, 836).

4. Another commentator added recently that "around [O'Connor] will eventually form a new and consistent majority on the affirmative action issue" (Haggard 1990, 50).

5. The only interest that justifies the use of racial classifications is the governmental interest in remedying the effects of "identified" as opposed to "societal discrimination" (Note 1991, 807, 828; Haggard 1990, 84). The substance of O'Connor's definition of permissible race-based classifications is discussed in this chapter.

6. *Shaw* has impelled the reconsideration of dozens of racially drawn electoral districts, designed to remedy conditions of racial vote dilution impermissible under the Voting Rights Act of 1965. See Grofman (1993), 1238; "Symposium" (1995). *Shaw*'s reevaluation of prior case law is discussed in this chapter.

7. The racial affirmative action line of cases dates back to the late 1970s, when the Burger Court first considered the constitutionality of benign or compensatory racial classifications. Such classifications, while limited in their application, were adjudged under a less exacting standard of equal protection review than those without an overtly beneficent purpose. This occurred in the now-landmark case of *Regents of the University of California v. Bakke* (438 U.S. 265, 1978). See also *United Steelworkers v. Weber* (443 U.S. 193, 1979).

The racial vote dilution line of cases begins even earlier, with the first challenges to "at-large" and multimember district elections under the Voting Rights Act of 1965. See *Allen v. State Board of Elections* (393 U.S. 544, 1969)(a section 5 preclearance case but the first to find at-large systems suspect); *Whitcomb v. Chavis* (403 U.S. 124, 1971); *White v. Regester* (412 U.S. 760, 1973). Because of the dilutionary effects of such districts on minority voting strength—caused by conditions of racial polarization in voting—the Court began to recommend the use of single-member districts drawn to reflect the racial composition of the electorate. For an early constitutional challenge to this practice, see *United Jewish Organization v. Carey* (430 U.S. 144, 1977).

8. It is important to point out that O'Connor's jurisprudence of community identity is not a communitarian jurisprudence, yet O'Connor has been called a kind of communitarian by one commentator who draws on her redistricting opinions as evidence. According to this commentator, O'Connor's opinions acknowledge "the priority of the community's interests, at the cost of diminishing the value of membership for some of its members," which "recalls the republican demand that individuals subordinate their selfish desires to the needs of the collective" (Sherry 1986, 598). This interpretation is somewhat

hard to square with O'Connor's own statements in her concurrence in the redistricting case of *Davis v. Bandemer* (478 U.S. 109, 149–51, 1986) and her antigroupism rhetoric in *Shaw*.

This communitarianism, this same commentator continues, reflects O'Connor's "feminine tendency to examine apportionment questions in context rather than in the abstract" (Sherry 1986, 598). There is nothing uniquely feminine about an anti-bright-line, contextualist approach to redistricting matters; however, feminine or not, this is an accurate description of O'Connor's approach.

9. The emergence of O'Connor's position on legally acknowledgeable communities of interest begins with a concurring statement in a case having nothing to do with race. O'Connor's ideas on the general nature of community identity and collective, community rights are rooted in her strong attachment to the principles of states' rights federalism. As was observed in chapter 2, O'Connor's pre-Supreme Court professional experience in state government helped to imbue her with a commitment to state sovereignty and local self-rule. As a justice, she is a well-known and outspoken defender of Tenth Amendment rights. See her opinions in *San Antonio Metropolitan Transit Authority v. Garcia* (469 U.S. 528, 1985), and *New York v. U.S.* (112 S.Ct. 2408, 1992). As a result, her juridical model for a "community of interest" is the geographic, governmental subdivision, a collective of citizens.

This perspective on community is apparent in one of the first opinions—a concurrence, as it happens—written by O'Connor. The opinion occurred in a 1981 case concerning a state revenue distribution scheme that relied on durational-residency classifications. Essentially, the state of Alaska relied on citizens' length of state residence to apportion varying dividends of a state resource fund; the Burger Court majority invalidated the distribution scheme as violating the equal protection clause (*Zobel v. Williams*, 457 U.S. 55 [1981]). O'Connor concurred in the judgment, but with two important and telling distinctions. First, she found it "neither inherently invidious or irrational" for a state to "desire to *compensate* citizens for their prior contributions" (457 U.S. at 72). As an example, she noted that a state could legitimately choose to divide its largesse among residents according to the number of years devoted to prior community service and volunteer community organizations (457 U.S. at 72, n. 1). She nevertheless objected to the distribution plan, because it afforded "a less valuable citizenship right" to newer as opposed to oldtime residents of the state, irrespective of any contributions made to the community. Because the plan established a situation in which "some groups of citizens who migrated to [the state] . . . *live in the state on less favorable terms* than those who arrived earlier," she found it in violation of the Privileges and Immunities of Citizens Clause of Article IV (457 U.S. at 75, 78; emphasis added).

The Alaska distribution case is interesting for two reasons: its early indication of the divergence between the conservative Justice Rehnquist, a dissentor, and his supposed "Arizona twin," concurror Justice O'Connor, and its revelation of the O'Connor philosophy of community rights and powers. In her opinion, O'Connor identified the community as a community of physical residency and cooperative reciprocity, made up of discrete, rights-bearing individuals whose interests are not subsumable within those of a group. In addition, the community of interest whose identity is at issue in the case is a governmental, territorial community. These elements of "community" have profoundly shaped O'Connor's consideration of the legal cognizability of other kinds of communities and their interests.

10. See the first draft of her concurrence in the judgment, 10 June 1986, p. 2, Marshall Papers, box 385, folder 10. Her statement on this matter continued: "generalizations, based on and qualified by the concrete situations that gave rise to them, must not be applied out of context in disregard of variant controlling facts."

11. 478 U.S. at 151 (emphasis added). Note memo of 15 January 1986, in which O'Connor tells White that she has "revisited" her position at conference on the justiciability of political gerrymanders. This memo contains some of the original language on the racial "nexus" that would find its way into the excerpted passage. See the memo noted above, p. 2, Marshall Papers, box 386, folder 1.

12. First, the minority group must be sufficiently large and geographically compact to constitute a majority in a single-member district. Second, the minority group must be politically cohesive in that a significant proportion of the group supports the same candidates. Third, the minority group must demonstrate that white majority bloc voting is of such a degree as to enable it to defeat consistently the minority's preferred candidates (478 U.S. at 30–34).

13. Interestingly, here, both the Brennan plurality and the O'Connor dissent claimed that they were each applying strict scrutiny to the plan, which both also agreed possessed a bona fide remedial purpose, but the record of conference memos shows that, from the outset, the two sides disagreed about the rigidity of the one-for-one system of relief. See O'Connor draft of 28 January 1987, Marshall Papers, box 415, folder 1, and Brennan draft of 29 January 1987, p. 30, n. 32, Marshall Papers, box 414, folder 11.

14. As O'Connor observed in her opinion, "we are a nation not of black and white alone, but one teeming with divergent *communities* knitted together by various traditions and carried forth, above all, by *individuals*." (497 U.S. 547, 610; 110 S.Ct. 2997, 3033 [1990]; emphasis added).

15. These include subdivision boundaries and integrity, but see Maveety (1991b), who notes that such concerns were not considered constitutionally requisite to secure "fair representation" according to the redistricting precedents of the Burger Court.

16. 113 S.Ct. at 2832. Interestingly, she gleaned this formulation from a *concurring opinion* filed in a 1977 racial gerrymandering case (opinion of White, *UJO v. Carey*, 430 U.S. at 167–68).

17. 113 S.Ct. at 2832. This is not to say that race-based districting plans could never survive close and exacting judicial scrutiny. As O'Connor made clear elsewhere in her decision, the intentional creation of majority-minority districts, *without more*, is not necessarily sufficient for an equal protection claim (113 S.Ct. at 2828), and she merely reaffirmed that racial-group political cohesion can never be assumed, but must be proved (113 S.Ct. at 2831).

Chapter Eight

Conclusion: Accommodationism and Quiet Leadership

... flexibility is a virtue and not a vice.

> —Justice Sandra Day O'Connor, concurring
> in *Capitol Square Review and Advisory
> Board v. Pinette* (1995)

The need for careful judgment and fine distinctions presents
itself even in extreme cases.

> —Justice Sandra Day O'Connor, concurring
> in *Rosenberger v. Rector and Visitors of
> the University of Virginia* (1995)

Capricious inattention has been paid to Justice O'Connor's role as a
doctrinal contributor and coalitional force on the later Burger and
contemporary Rehnquist Courts. Perhaps because she has served
alongside more ideologically defined judges such as Justices Brennan,
Marshall, Rehnquist, and Scalia, her contextualizing approach has
frequently been overshadowed by the sheer drama of her colleagues'
rhetoric. Many court commentators, too, seem to have been blinded
by her status as a "famous first" and have persistently viewed O'Connor's work through the lens of "women's interests." Not only is this
approach inapt with respect to O'Connor the jurist, it has occasioned
scholarly oversight of the truly salient and, arguably, revolutionary
characteristics of O'Connor the judicial actor. Such oversight has been
directly related to a failure to appreciate the emergence of her quiet
leadership style and the importance of her post-legal realist use of case
facts. Both have had a profound effect on the Court's interworkings
and outputs.

127

"Quiet" is possibly the wrong adjective for O'Connor's leadership style, because its unconventionality as a strategy for influence—at least in the judicial setting—has attracted critical attention from court colleagues and court commentators alike.[1] "Quiet" nevertheless seems to describe the way O'Connor's subtle influence on the Court's output—exercised through jurisprudential and behavioral accommodationism—subverts traditional canons of leadership. Her leadership style is distinctive for its utilization of a new, more choral convention of cooperative decision-making and doctrinal production. As such, it is a tactic of influence that fosters submergence in a coalition. In examining a judge like O'Connor, who votes fairly faithfully with the ideologically conservative bloc in many issue areas such as criminal procedure and federalism[2], the tendency is to assume that even in areas where she shows more independence in terms of voting and opinion content, she is still best described as a coalition partner, not a coalition leader. She has, however, been a leader in using the factual content of cases as a means of generating and applying new, flexible judicial standards. Her jurisprudential accommodationism leads her to author narrow, fact-specific rulings that fine-tune a majority position, and her behavioral accommodationism leads her to retain majority-side membership and speak through the "concurring voice." These decisional attributes are somewhat "risk-adverse" strategies for influence over the court's collective output, but they seem also to be conscious choices to pursue incremental and collegial methods for legal change. Even so, her judicial accommodationism is not readily recognized as leadership, quiet or otherwise.

O'Connor's juridical record should be reevaluated also in light of her exercise of nontraditional, quasilegislative approaches to judicial policy making. This approach includes a post-legal realist view of case facts where case facts are used to contextualize case situations and to contextually apply doctrinal rules.[3] Of necessity, then, O'Connor's judicial standards are somewhat imprecise and unsystematic, and, while the results they yield are often conservative, they are not uniformly so. Arguably, O'Connor's opposition to ideological judging is a return to the commonsense conservatism of a Justice Harlan; in this way, she offers the Rehnquist Court an alternative conservative personality. Some, however, would deride her approach as "fingers-to-the-wind" jurisprudence, because it seems so nakedly results and compromise oriented. Indeed, one journalist comments that it is striking how much the Rehnquist Court's "swing justices"—he names O'Connor among them—"want to remain followers, not leaders, in our national political debates" (Toobin 1995, 82). O'Connor, it seems, can be criticized for being both too political and not political enough; yet, clearly, her judicial flexibility is an unavoidable consequence of her post-legal realist approach to case facts and her avoidance of ideological, categorical rules. Whether excessively or insufficiently political, her accommodationism constitutes a jurisprudence.

In a recent concurring judgment, O'Connor summarized both her juridical method and her differences with some of her Rehnquist Court colleagues.

> When bedrock principles collide, they test the limits of categorical obstinacy and expose the flaws and dangers of a Grand Unified Theory that may turn out to be neither grand nor unified.[4]

O'Connor shows every sign of continuing her judicial accommodationism, even in the face of stinging attacks from the conservative wing of the Court, led by Justice Scalia;[5] indeed, O'Connor's identification of "categorical obstinacy" and "Grand Unified Theory" in the above quote is arguably an uncomplimentary reference to Scalia's creation of per se rules. The context of this retort was the familiar yet perennially contested territory of establishment clause jurisprudence—debate over which dominated two closely decided and high-profile cases from the 1994–1995 term.[6]

A select survey of this past term reveals the strengths and weaknesses of O'Connor's strategic accommodationism, as well as offering a prognosis for its future. In terms of behavioral accommodationism and majority-side alliance, O'Connor was part of five-member majorities in three highly publicized decisions. She joined the most conservative wing of the Court in the revolutionary ruling in *U.S. v. Lopez*, which held that a federal statute outlawing firearm possession near schools exceeded the scope of the power to regulate interstate commerce.[7] She also joined the decision in the voting rights case of *Miller v. Johnson*, in which five members of the Court ("evaluating the showing of bizarreness" in redistricting plans) held that minority-majority electoral districts are unconstitutional if race was the dominant reason for drawing the district lines (63 LW 4726, 1995). Her brief concurrence merely emphasized that the *Miller* Court was following the standard[8] laid out by her own opinion for the Court in *Shaw v. Reno* (63 LW at 4736). Finally, she seems to have been the swing vote in *Rosenberger v. University of Virginia*, in which the Court upheld the First Amendment speech rights of a student religious group and held that university funding of the group's newspaper would not violate the establishment clause (63 LW 4702, 1995). Here, a somewhat lengthier O'Connor concurrence explained the ruling in terms of "endorsement," while observing that "[e]xperience proves that the Establishment clause, like the Free speech clause, cannot easily be reduced to a single test" (63 LW at 4710, 4712). In all three cases, the same coalition of Stevens, Souter, Ginsburg, and Breyer dissented— illustrating, perhaps, O'Connor's potential estrangement from the Rehnquist Court's more moderate wing. O'Connor's jurisprudential accommodationism of the past term would, however, seem to tell a different story, as is seen in the intra-Court argument over *Capitol Square Review and Advisory Board v. Pinette.*

The *Capitol Square* case once again found the Court battling over the establishment clause and the endorsement principle; however, unlike past cases in which O'Connor's endorsement test existed at the margins of official legal doctrine, in *Capitol Square* the meaning and application of the endorsement test was at the center of a pitched battle between Scalia, O'Connor, Souter, and Stevens. A plurality of the Court, led by Scalia, held that no violation of the establishment clause occurred when the Klu Klux Klan was granted a permit to engage in private religious expression on a statehouse plaza, even though the expression consisted of the display of an unattended cross. Key to the plurality was the fact that the square was a public forum, open to the public for speech through a neutral permit application process. O'Connor, joined by Souter and Breyer, concurred in the ruling, although she parted company with the Scalia opinion over the application of the endorsement test. Arguing that the endorsement test had no application to private speech, even that sanctioned by the government, Scalia dismissed the test as "supply[ing] no standard whatsoever" (63 LW 4684, 4688, n. 3). Defending the endorsement test, O'Connor observed that "the Establishment Clause inquiry cannot be distilled into a fixed, per se rule, [for] every government practice must be judged in its *unique circumstances* to determine whether it constitutes an endorsement or disapproval of religion" (63 LW at 4691; emphasis added). Further defending the flexibility of her establishment clause standard, O'Connor added the idea that "the endorsement test necessarily focuses upon the perception of a reasonable, informed observer" (63 LW at 4689). This doctrinal refinement received the endorsement of Souter in his concurring opinion, which O'Connor and Breyer also joined (63 LW at 4693–95).

Three things are apparent in *Capitol Square*. First, even though the

Scalia plurality eventually delimited the application of the endorsement test, his opinion is a de facto assumption that the test is now central to establishment clause jurisprudence and therefore must be rebutted. Second, far from signifying estrangement, the coalitional alignment of the *Capitol Square* Court suggests that O'Connor's alliance with the moderately conservative center justices remains intact. Third, the very porousness of O'Connor's doctrinal standard led to an outcome in which several factions of the Court all had a different interpretation of "endorsement." While the dissent in the case cited with authority O'Connor's endorsement "precedents" (some, after all, are "mere" concurring opinions), the content of Stevens's dissenting opinion reveals his distance from O'Connor's conception of the reasonable observer under the endorsement test. Stevens argued that O'Connor had relied on an "ideal observer" who "comes off as a well-schooled jurist" judging endorsement in order to reach her decision in the case (63 LW at 4697, n. 5). The *Capitol Square* debate thus reveals both the strength and the weakness of O'Connor's jurisprudential accommodationism: the flexibility of her judicial standards encourages their acceptance as Court doctrine, but that same flexiblity means that any faction of the Court can use her language—perhaps as a way of enticing O'Connor's vote—without losing anything by way of substance or preferred outcome.

Do O'Connor's rule aversion, contextualist use of facts, and risk-adverse influence tactics then threaten to undermine the utility of her judicial accommodationism? What is its projected future as an attractive option for marshaling the Court? As has been discussed, O'Connor's pragmatic centrism, both in voting and in jurisprudence, was a viable influence strategy during the Burger years, when the Court was gripped by an entrenched, ideological polarization. The strategy has remained viable on the Rehnquist Court, which has suffered from a jurisprudential polarization (the so-called justices of rules versus justices of standards division) among an increasingly ideologically similar judicial cohort. The Ginsburg and Breyer appointments, as well as the apparently leftward drift of Bush-appointee Souter, suggest a change in the Court's ideological composition. If the Rehnquist Court enters a period of renewed liberal-conservative (ideological) polarization while retaining cross-cutting cleavages of jurisprudential polarization, O'Connor's influential position would seem to continue. As the *Capitol Square* example would seem to indicate, however, general adoption of O'Connor's judicial standards does not mean that the Court will speak with her voice or that its policy direction will become more focused.

Indeed, O'Connor's anti-bright-line jurisprudential approach increases the avenues for judicial discretion and messy case-by-case analysis of constitutional questions, yet O'Connor brings a genuinely conservative outlook to questions of legal and policy change; as long as the Court's composition retains a conservative to moderately conservative orientation, the Court's application of O'Connor's doctrinal standards will as well. A Court marshaled by judicial accommodationism thus would probably retain the separate opinion writing behavior so favored by O'Connor as an important method for securing doctrinal change. It is fair, therefore, to claim that an O'Connor-led Court would be generally conservative, but conservative because of careful fact-based balancing, not doctrinaire rule following.

This study accepts as irrefutable that O'Connor's conservative pattern of voting behavior conforms in many respects with the expectations of the attitudinal model of the judicial process. What this analysis offers is a complement to the ideological or attitude-driven model of judging, for that model cannot capture all aspects of judicial action, particularly those that relate to interjudicial influence, fluidity, and the multidimensional character of judicial choice (Epstein and Knight, 1995). An important aspect of O'Connor's contribution to the Court is thus not captured by a unidimensional attitudinal profile. The evidence necessary to make this claim is largely qualitative and based on content analysis of opinions, which raises certain issues of methodological compatibility with the behavioral presumptions of the attitudinal model; but simply because evidentiary factors are not measured quantitatively and relationships among them are not assessed in terms of aggregate data analysis, there is no reason to dismiss the evidence as spurious. As the practitioners of neoinstitutionalism in judicial studies posit, "qualitative studies of the patterns of reasoning characteristic of various strains of legal discourse [are] investigations into one dimension of actual political conduct," a dimension that is empirically relevant in that "judicial decision makers often have a range of choice on how to advance the interests and principles they perceive as imperative" (Smith 1988, 90, 99).

The above observation suggests a certain impossibility to systematic analysis of judicial decision-making. If "systematic" is defined as identifying all possible independent variables that determine judicial choice and as specifying those variables in a way that permits exacting assessment of relationships among variables, then no analysis can hope to capture the complexity of reality. Even the most rigorous judicial behaviorists, however, do not make such claims about their methods. Quantitative, systematic analysis must always be supplemented and informed by qualitative, even intuitive, studies of judging and of the judicial decision-making context. This was (and remains) the role played by judicial biography in the public law subfield—indeed, the promise of the neoinstitutionalist perspective on the judicial process lies in its (re)appreciation of the complexity of the phenomena it purports to describe and explain.

This study hopes to contribute modestly to a richer neo-institutionalist appreciation of the Supreme Court decision-making environment. It is probably too early to say whether O'Connor's judicial behavior is either idiosyncratic and ultimately forgettable or indicative of a larger trend regarding decision-making conventions on the modern Court, but the nature and impact of her brand of judicial accommodationism is not susceptible at this stage to analysis that follows the reductionist assumptions of the attitudinal model. The goal of qualitative work about the Court is to identify and isolate variables that might later be amenable to more systematic, quantitative analyses of the judicial process.

One schema developed by such qualitative work is the distinction between institutional and individualistic styles of judging (Bennett 1991). These styles are a matter of judicial role orientation, not the ideological substance of a judge's views. The styles differ across two dimensions: that of separate opinion issuance and that of obedience to precedent in decisions. Institutional behavior by judges is thus both horizontal and vertical: the former concerns dealing with one's colleagues and searching for consensus in the collegial decision-making enterprise; the latter concerns dealing with precedent and the norm of stare decisis (Bennett 1991, 256). Can O'Connor be placed in this schema, contemplating the decline of consensual norms on the modern Court, especially since the post-Warren era (Walker, Epstein, and Dixon 1988)? If the contemporary Court is too far toward the individualistic judging style—on both dimensions (Bennett 1991, 258)—then is O'Connor's judicial accommodationism detrimental to the institutional norms of the Court? She is arguably an institutionalist across the vertical dimension (precedent), but seems patently individualistic across the horizontal dimension (separate opinion writing). How, then, should her record be assessed?

There is, arguably, an important institutional or consensus-building purpose served by separate opinions, particularly the first time the issue arises. This is to sharpen the alternative position and argument (Bennett 1991, 259). Dissents are traditionally viewed in this way, although repeated and repetitious dissent allegedly drains the device of its power through overuse; but concurrence—to paraphrase a commentator—is closer to a form of "tactical acquiescence," for the concurror leaves undisturbed the decision coalition (though perhaps not the opinion coalition) until such time that "he can find a majority for a view he never abandoned in his heart" (Bennett 1991, 260). Viewed in this way, concurring-opinion issuance looks like an inventive method of behaving institutionally across the horizontal dimension of judging.

In the case data analyzed here, O'Connor's concurrence, as well as her jurisprudential accommodationism, has had a constructive effect on constitutional law. In the three closely examined issue areas— church-state relations, abortion rights, and race-based equal protection—her actions have moved the Court toward a consensus. Two points might be made here. First, appointment factors are hardly irrelevant in shaping consensus on the Court. As mentioned above, the emergence of a "second Burger Court," with the formation of the moderate-liberal axis of Ginsburg, Souter, Breyer, and Stevens, is certainly a possibility and has implications for coalition behavior—and for O'Connor's overtures from the center—in the future. Second, O'Connor is clearly not the first judge to use concurrence, though she is one of the few to use it in such a sustained and consistent fashion. This latter point lends credence to the assertion that O'Connor's use of separate opinions to bracket rulings of the majority is a contemporary inauguration of the seriatim opinion method, making allowance for the fact that majority opinions of the Court remain the modern decision-making convention.

Obviously, a small sample of the decisional record of one justice is hardly definitive evidence of a macro trend, but it is suggestive. What it suggests is that O'Connor's style of judging is the model that now shapes the Supreme Court's collective decision-making process, implying a profound revision of what it means to be a "judicial conservative" and a profound revision of the judicial process on collegial courts. Clearly, judicial conservatives are capable of doctrinal as well as institutional innovations. To describe a Court—such as the Rehnquist Court—as dominated by judicial conservatives, is therefore merely the beginning of the inquiry. The definition of "collegiality" on collective decision-making bodies, moreover, such as multimember courts, may require some reevalution in light of the contemporary phenomenon of decision-making and doctrinal production through issuing multiple opinions. In precipitating such developments and reassessments of the judicial institution, perhaps O'Connor is a "famous first" after all.

Notes

1. Commentators Segal and Spaeth chastise O'Connor for her propensity to switch sides and break up decisional coalitions, as well as for her willingness to disregard and/or tinker with precedent. Similarly, colleagues such as Scalia continue to rail against the "so-called endorsement test," for example, as evidence of her judicial apostasy (see Scalia's plurality opinion in *Capitol Square Review and Advisory Board v. Pinette*, 63 LW 4684, 4686 [1995]).

2. See Cook (1991) pp. 250–57; Wermiel (1991) pp. 139–40, but cf. *Vernonia School District v. Acton* (63 LW 4653, 1995) (O'Connor, J., dissenting from ruling that random, suspicionless urinalysis of school athletes for drug use is not unreasonable under the Fourth Amendment) and *Edmonds v. Oxford House* (63 LW 4402, 1995) (O'Connor joining majority finding that local zoning definition of a "family" is not exempt from federal FHA antidiscrimination provisions).

3. This suggests interesting work for fact pattern analysis, addressing, among other questions, whether O'Connor reads facts selectively and responds to them accordingly.

A recent study of the modern Court argues that the Rehnquist period has inaugurated an era of "restraintist realism," by which is meant (1) a deference to the judgments of elected officials because of their presumed competence and (2) an assumption of policy-making competence by judges through the use of techniques such as balancing of interests, which partake of the legislative method (Faille 1995, 167, 29). Such restraintist realism would seem to comport with O'Connor's "post-legal realism" with respect to case facts, although it should be pointed out that the author of the aforementioned study did not intend the term as a compliment.

4. *Rosenberger v. Rector and Visitors of the University of Virginia*, 63 LW 4702, 4712 (1995) (O'Connor, J., concurring). In a 5–4 decision, the Court held that a state university violated the First Amendment's speech clause in refusing to fund the newspaper of a school religious group and would not violate the establishment clause by funding religious speech. O'Connor's divergence from the Court's view turned on the application of the concept of "endorsement" (at 4710). Arguably, O'Connor was the critical fifth vote in upholding the rights of the religious school newspaper, since her sometime allies, moderates Souter and Breyer, as well as the more liberal moderates Stevens and Ginsburg, dissented.

5. Such intra-Court intrigue has been detailed recently by Simon (1995).

6. *Capitol Square Review and Advisory Board v. Pinette*, 63 LW 4684 (1995); *Rosenberger v. University of Virginia*, 63 LW 4702 (1995).

7. 63 LW 4343 (1995). O'Connor reaffirmed her alliance with the conservative, states-rights wing of the Court in *Lopez* and in *U.S. Term Limits v. Thornton* (63 LW 4413, 1995), in which she joined the four-member dissent, which vigorously defended a Tenth Amendment basis for state-authorized term limits for members of Congress. In neither case, however, did she author her own concurring or dissenting opinion; moreover, her alliance with the most ideologically conservative justices remains irregular, as is evidenced by her dissent from the Court's decision in *Vernonia School District v. Acton*. O'Connor, joined by Stevens and Souter, dissented from the Court's ruling that random, suspicionless urinalysis of school athletes for drug use was not unreasonable under the Fourth Amendment (63 LW 4653, 4659 [1995]).

8. Pamela Karlan argues that this "standard" is no standard at all, but a reinvocation of "I know it when I see it" jurisprudence. See Karlan (1995).

Appendix

Justice Sandra Day O'Connor Interview Questions[1]

1. Prior to your appointment to the Supreme Court, you had held positions at all three levels of government in the state of Arizona. To what extent did any or all of these positions prepare you for being a Supreme Court justice? What, if any, experiences in government, private practice, or education do you believe are good preparation for an individual to be a Supreme Court justice?

2. Is there a typical stage in the decisional process where you make the decision to either write or not write a separate opinion? For example, is the decision made after the conference proceedings, or after reading a draft of the majority opinion, or after reading another separate opinion? Is the stage the same regardless of the type of separate opinion that you are considering?

3. Why do you write separate opinions in some cases? Are the reasons the same regardless of the type of separate opinion (dissenting, concurring) that you author? Why might you withdraw a separate opinion after you were planning to file such an opinion in a case?

4. In a case where you have been assigned the majority opinion and there is expressed disagreement on the reasoning and/or outcome of the decision among your brethren, how do you address and deal with that disagreement in the preparation of your opinion? How does your approach compare to those used by the other justices in the same type of situation?

5. In a case where you are a member of the majority, do you have the discretion to indicate to the Chief Justice or the senior justice making the assignment of the majority opinion that you would prefer

not to author the Court's opinion in such a case? During your tenure on the Court, have you ever exercised such discretion? If so, why?

6. Judges, lawyers, and scholars have long debated how an eighteenth-century Constitution should be understood and applied to contemporary issues. In a case where a legal question involves the interpretation of a constitutional phrase, what approach do you take to resolve the meaning and application of the phrase to a modern-day problem?

7. Although not as intense, there is also a debate on how statutes should be understood and applied to current issues that fall outside the scope of the laws as written. In a case involving the interpretation of a federal statute to address either a situation, activity, or group of people clearly not listed in the law, what approach do you take to resolve the meaning and application of the federal law? Is that approach similar or dissimilar to the approach that you would take in dealing with a state statute or local ordinance?

8. Are you aware of any media accounts or scholarly writings that contained important misconceptions about your Court service? If so, in what ways are these accounts or writings in error?

Notes

1. These questions were submitted to Justice O'Connor for written response in July 1993 by Prof. Robert C. Bradley, as part of a joint project undertaken with the author. O'Connor's answers are incorporated in the text. Text of the responses to particular questions is available upon request.

Bibliography

Abel, Richard. 1989. *American Lawyers*. New York: Oxford University Press.

Abraham, Henry. 1985. *Justices and Presidents*. New York: Oxford University Press.

Allen, Anita. 1992. "Autonomy's Magic Wand: Abortion and Constitutional Interpretation." *Boston University Law Review* 72: 683–98.

Altfeld, Michael, and Harold Spaeth. 1984. "Measuring Influence on the U.S. Supreme Court." *Jurimetrics Journal* 24: 236–47.

Axelrod, Robert. 1970. *Conflict of Interest*. Chicago: Markham.

Bartlett, Katherine, and Roseann Kennedy. 1991. *Feminist Legal Thought*. Boulder, Colo.: Westview.

Baum, Lawrence. 1989. *The Supreme Court*. Washington, D.C.: Congressional Quarterly.

———— 1992. "Membership Change and Collective Voting Change in the U.S. Supreme Court." *Journal of Politics* 54: 3–21.

Behuniak-Long, Susan. 1992. "Justice Sandra Day O'Connor and the Power of Maternal Thinking." *The Review of Politics* 1992: 417–44.

Bennett, Robert W. 1991. "A Dissent on Dissent." *Judicature* 74: 255–60.

Bertz, Randall. 1992. "Abortion 1990s: Contemporary Issues and the Activist Court." *Western State University Law Review* 19: 393–429.

BeVier, Lillian R. 1992. "Rehabilitating Public Forum Doctrine: A Defense of Categories." *Supreme Court Review* 1992: 79–122.

Blasi, Vincent. 1983. "The Rootless Activism of the Burger Court." In *The Burger Court: The Counterrevolution That Wasn't*, ed. V. Blasi, 198–217. New Haven, Conn.: Yale University Press.

Blumrosen, Alfred W. 1991. "Society in Transition III: Justice O'Connor and the Destabilization of the *Griggs* Principle of Employment Discrimination." *Women's Rights Law Reporter* 13: 53–70.

Bodine, Laurence. 1983. "Sandra Day O'Connor." *ABA Journal* 69: 1395–98.

Brace, Paul, and Melinda Gann Hall. 1993. "Integrated Models of Judicial Dissent." *Journal of Politics* 55: 914–35.

Bibliography

Bradley, Robert C., and Nancy Maveety. 1992a. "The Occurrence of Concurrence: Correlates of Justice O'Connor's Concurring Opinions." A paper presented to the annual meeting of the American Political Science Association, Chicago, 3–6 September 1992.

——— 1992b. "Reductionist Conservatism: the Judicial Ideology of Justice Sandra Day O'Connor." *Quarterly Journal of Ideology* 15: 45–62.

Brennan, William J. 1986. "In Defense of Dissent." *Hastings Law Journal* 37: 427–38.

Brenner, Saul. 1989. "Fluidity on the U.S. Supreme Court: A Reexamination." In *American Court Systems*, ed. S. Goldman and A. Sarat, 479–85. White Plains, N.Y.: Longman.

Brenner, Saul, and Harold Spaeth. 1990a. "Ideological Position as a Variable in the Authoring of Dissenting Opinions on the Warren and Burger Courts." In *Studies in U.S. Supreme Court Behavior*, ed. H. Spaeth and S. Brenner, 279–89. New York: Garland.

——— 1990b. "Majority Opinion Assignments and the Maintenance of the Original Coalition on the Warren Court." In *Studies in U.S. Supreme Court Behavior*, ed. H. Spaeth and S. Brenner, 123–35. New York: Garland.

Brisbin, Richard. 1989. "Conservative Jurisprudence in the Reagan Era." *Cumberland Law Review* 19: 497–537.

——— 1990. "The Conservatism of Antonin Scalia." *Political Science Quarterly* 105: 1–29.

Cameron, Charles. 1993. "New Avenues for Modeling Judicial Politics." A paper presented to the 2d annual meeting of the Conference on the Political Economy of Public Law, University of Rochester, Rochester, N.Y., 15–16 October 1993.

Cameron, Charles, Jeffrey Segal, and Donald Songer. 1993. "Law Creation and Signaling in the Judicial Hierarchy." Unpublished paper, 9 March 1993.

Chemerinsky, Erwin. 1989. "Forward: The Vanishing Constitution." *Harvard Law Review* 103: 43–104.

Cook, Beverly B. 1991. "Justice Sandra Day O'Connor: Transition to a Republican Court Agenda. In *The Burger Court: Political and Judicial Profiles*, ed. C. Lamb and S. Halpern, 238–75. Urbana and Champaign, Ill.: University of Illinois Press.

Craig, Barbara Hinkson, and David M. O'Brien. 1993. *Abortion and American Politics*. Chatham, N.J.: Chatham House.

Danelski, David J. 1968. "The Influence of the Chief Justice in the Decision Process of the Supreme Court." In *The Federal Judicial System*, ed. T. Jahnige and S. Goldman. New York: Holt, Rinehart, and Winston.

——— 1973. "Conflict and Its Resolution in the Supreme Court." In *American Judicial Behavior*, ed. S. Brenner. New York: MSS.

Danelski, David J., and Jeanne C. Danelski. 1989. "Leadership in the Warren Court." In *American Court Systems*, ed. S. Goldman and A. Sarat, 500–19. New York: Longman.

Davidson, Chandler. 1984. "Minority Vote Dilution: An Overview." In *Minority Vote Dilution*, ed. C. Davidson, 1–41. Washington, D.C.: Howard University Press.

Davis, Sue. 1989. *Justice Rehnquist and the Constitution*. Princeton, N.J.: Princeton University Press.

——— 1990. "Power on the Court: Chief Justice Rehnquist's Opinion Assignments." *Judicature* 74: 66–72.

——— 1993. "The Voice of Sandra O'Connor." *Judicature* 77: 134–39.

Denniston, Lyle. 1995. "The Pivotal Vote." *The Baltimore Sun* (1 October 1995): 1.

Ellman, Faye. 1992/3. "Lawyer of the Year: Sandra Day O'Connor." *National Law Journal* (28 December 1992–4 January 1993): 1.

Epstein, Lee, and Jack Knight. 1995. "Documenting Strategic Interaction on the U.S. Supreme Court." A paper presented to the Annual Meeting of the American Political Science Association, Chicago, 31 August–3 September 1995.

Epstein, Lee, and Joseph Kobylka. 1992. *The Supreme Court and Legal Change*. Chapel Hill, N.C.: University of North Carolina Press.

Epstein, Lee, and Thomas G. Walker. 1992. *Constitutional Law for a Changing America: Rights, Liberties, and Justice*. Washington, D.C.: Congressional Quarterly Press.

Eskridge, William, Jr., and John Ferejohn. 1992. "The Article I, Section 7 Game." *Georgetown Law Journal* 80: 523–64.

Eskridge, William, Jr., and Philip Frickey. 1988. *Cases and Materials on Legislation: Statutes and the Creation of Public Policy*. St. Paul, Minn.: West.

Faille, Christopher C. 1995. *The Decline and Fall of the Supreme Court*. Westport, Conn.: Praeger.

Feder, Benjamin. 1988. "And a Child Shall Lead Them: Justice O'Connor, the Principle of Religious Liberty, and Its Practical Application." *Pace Law Review* 8: 249–302.

Ferejohn, John, and Barry Weingast. 1992. "A Positive Theory of Statutory Interpretation." *International Review of Law and Economics* 12: 263–79.

Gelfand, M. David, and Keith Werhan. 1990. "Federalism and Separation of Powers on a 'Conservative' Court: Currents and Crosscurrents from Justices O'Connor and Scalia." *Tulane Law Review* 64: 1443–76.

Gerber, Scott, and Keeok Park. 1994. "The Search for Consensus on the U.S. Supreme Court: A Cross-Judicial Case Study of the Rehnquist Court." A paper presented to the Annual Meeting of the Southern Political Science Association, Atlanta, Ga., 2–4 November 1994.

Gibson, James L. 1991. "Decision Making in Appellate Courts." In *The American Courts: a Critical Perspective*, ed. J. Gates and C. Johnson, 255–78. Washington, D.C.: Congressional Quarterly Press.

Ginsburg, Ruth Bader. 1990. "Remarks on Writing Separately." *Washington Law Review* 65: 133–50.

Goldman, Sheldon, and Thomas Jahnige. 1985. *The Federal Courts as a Political System* (3d ed.) New York: Harper and Row.

Graglia, Lino. 1988. "The 'Remedy' Rationale for Requiring or Permitting Otherwise Prohibited Discrimination: How the Court Overcame the Constitution and the 1964 Civil Rights Act." *Suffolk Law Review* 22: 569–605.

Greenhouse, Linda. 1992. "Liberal Giants Inspire Three Centrist Justices." *New York Times* (25 October 1992): 1.

Grofman, Bernard. 1982. "A Dynamic Model of Proto-Coalition Formation in Ideological N-Space." *Behavioral Science* 27: 77–90.

———— 1993. "Would Vince Lombardi Have Been Right if He Had Said: 'When It Comes to Redistricting, Race Isn't Everything, It's the Only Thing'?" *Cardozo Law Review* 14: 1237–76.

———— 1995. "*Shaw v. Reno* and the Future of Voting Rights." *PS: Political Science and Politics* 28: 27–36.

Haggard, Thomas R. 1990. "Mugwump, Mediator, Machiavellian, or Majority? The Role of Justice O'Connor in the Affirmative Action Cases." *Akron Law Review* 24: 47–87.

Hagle, Timothy, and Harold Spaeth. 1991. "Voting Fluidity and the Attitudinal Model of Supreme Court Decision Making." *Western Political Quarterly* 44: 119–28.

———— 1992. "A Validity Test for Inferring Judicial Attitudes from Individual Voting Behavior." A paper presented to the annual meeting of the American Political Science Association, Chicago, 3–6 September 1992.

Haynie, Stacia L. 1989. "The Collapse of Consensus on the U.S. Supreme Court: Dissenting Votes or a Matter of Opinion?" A paper presented to the annual meeting of the American Political Science Association, Atlanta, 31 August–3 September 1989.

———— 1992. "Leadership and Consensus on the U.S. Supreme Court." *Journal of Politics* 54: 1158–69.

Hearings before the Senate Judiciary Committee on the Nomination of Judge Sandra Day O'Connor of Arizona to Serve as an Associate Justice of the Supreme Court of the U.S., 97th Cong., 1st sess. (1981).

Heck, Ed, and Paula Arledge. 1986. "Justice O'Connor and the First Amendment." *Pepperdine Law Review* 13: 993–1019.

Horner, Matina S. 1990. *Sandra Day O'Connor*. New York: Chelsea House.

Howard, J. Woodford. 1968. "On the Fluidity of Judicial Choice." *American Political Science Review* 62: 43–56.

Johnson, Philip. 1984. "Concept as Compromise: First Amendment Religious Doctrine." *California Law Review* 72: 817–46.

Jonasdottir, Anna. 1988. "On the Concept of Interest, Women's Interests, and the Limitations of Interest Theory." In *The Political Interests of Gender*, ed. K. Jones and A. Jonasdottir, 33–65. London: Sage.

Kahn, Ronald, 1994. *The Supreme Court and Constitutional Theory*. Lawrence, Kans.: University of Kansas Press.

Karlan, Pamela. 1993. "All over the Map: The Supreme Court's Voting Rights Trilogy." *Supreme Court Review* 1993: 245–87.

———— 1995. "Still Hazy After All These Years: Voting Rights in The Post *Shaw* Era." A Paper Presented to the Annual Meeting of The American Political Science Association, Chicago, 31 August–3 September 1995.

Kelman, Maurice. 1986. "The Forked Path of Dissent." *Supreme Court Review* 1985: 227–98.

Kohn, Howard. 1993. "Front and Center: Sandra Day O'Connor." *Los Angeles Times Magazine* (18 April 1993): 14–61.

Kornhauser, Lewis, and Lawrence Sager. 1993. "The One and the Many: Adjudication in Collegial Courts." *California Law Review* 81: 1–59.

Levinson, Sandford. 1994. "Identifying the Compelling State Interest: On 'Due Process of Lawmaking' and the Professional Responsibility of the Public Lawyer." A paper presented to the Conference on Reconciling Public Values and Individual Rights in Constitutional Adjudication. Hastings College of the Law, San Francisco, Calif., 26 February 1994.

Levy, Leonard. 1986. *The Establishment Clause: Religion and the First Amendment.* New York: Macmillan.

Marshall Papers (Collected Papers of Thurgood Marshall, Associate Justice of the U.S. Supreme Court), U.S. Library of Congress.

Maveety, Nancy. 1987. "The Populist of the Adversary Society: the Jurisprudence of Justice Rehnquist." *Journal of Contemporary Law* 13: 221–47.

———— 1989. "The Effect of Corporate Litigants on Free Speech Doctrine." A paper presented to the annual meeting of the Southern Political Science Association, Memphis, Tenn., 2–4 November 1989.

———— 1991a. "The Judicial Strategy of the Concurring Opinion." A paper presented to the annual meeting of the American Political Science Association, Washington, D.C., 29 August–1 September 1991.

———— 1991b. *Representation Rights and the Burger Years.* Ann Arbor, Mich.: University of Michigan Press.

———— 1994. "Strategic Interaction on Collegial Courts." A paper presented to the Conference on Constitutions and Constitutionalism, Murphy Institute of Political Economy, Tulane University, New Orleans, La., 18–20 February 1994.

Maveety, Nancy, and Robert C. Bradley. 1993. "Justice O'Connor: A Different Kind of Court Leader?" *Southeastern Political Review* 21: 39–57.

McGough, Michael. 1990. "Menorah Wars." *The New Republic* (5 February 1990): 12–14.

Murphy, Walter. 1964. *Elements of Judicial Strategy.* Chicago: University of Chicago Press.

———— 1966. "Courts as Small Groups," *Harvard Law Review* 79: 1565–1603.

N.A. 1987. "Women Judges: Tokens or Outsiders?" *Justice System Journal* 12: 232–44.

Note. 1985a. "The Emerging Jurisprudence of Justice O'Connor." *University of Chicago Law Review* 52: 389–459.

Note. 1985b. "Justice O'Connor: Token or Triumph from a Feminist Perspective?" *Golden Gate Law Review* 15: 493–525.

Note. 1987. "The Conservative as Liberal: The Religion Clauses, Liberal Neutrality, and the Approach of Justice O'Connor." *Notre Dame Law Review* 62: 151–91.

Note. 1989. "Sandra Day O'Connor, Abortion, and Compromise for the Court." *Touro Law Review* 5: 327–49.

Note. 1991. "Affirmative Action: Will Justice O'Connor Author Its End?" *Toledo Law Review* 22: 805–37.

Note. 1993. "Justices Harlan and Black Revisited: The Emerging Dispute between Justice O'Connor and Justice Scalia over Unenumerated Fundamental Rights." *Fordham Law Review* 61: 895–933.

Note. 1994. "Failing Honorably: Balancing Tests, Justice O'Connor, and Free Exercise of Religion." *St. Louis University Law Review* 38: 837–79.

O'Brien, David M. 1990. *Storm Center*. New York: W.W. Norton.

——— 1991. *Constitutional Law and Politics, Vol. 2*. New York: W.W. Norton.

O'Connor, Karen, and Jeffrey Segal. 1990. "Justice Sandra Day O'Connor and the Supreme Court's Reaction to Its First Female Member." In *Women, Politics, and the Constitution*, ed. N. Lynn, 95–104. New York: Harrington Park.

O'Connor, Sandra Day. 1981. "Trends in the Relationship between Federal and State Courts from the Perspective of a State Court Judge." *William and Mary Law Review* 22: 801–19.

——— 1984. "Our Judicial Federalism." *Case Western Reserve Law Review* 35: 1–21.

——— 1985. "Achievements of Women in the Legal Profession." *New York State Bar Journal* 1985: 8–10.

——— 1990. "Women and the Constitution: A Bicentennial Perspective." In *Women, Politics, and the Constitution*, ed. N. Lynn, 5–16. New York: Harrington Park.

——— 1991. "Madison Lecture: Portia's Progress." *New York University Law Review* 66: 1546–58.

——— 1992. "Keynote Address: Conference on Compelling Government Interests." *Albany Law Review* 55: 538–47.

——— 1993. Interview with Professor Robert C. Bradley (letter of 1 September 1993).

Palmer, Barbara. 1991. "Feminist or Foe? Justice Sandra Day O'Connor, Title VII Sex-Discrimination, and Support for Women's Rights." *Women's Rights Law Reporter* 13: 159–70.

Parker, Frank. 1990. *Black Votes Count*. Chapel Hill, N.C.: University of North Carolina Press.

Peterson, Steven A. 1981. "Dissent in American Courts." *Journal of Politics* 43: 412–34.

Ray, Laura Krugman. 1990. "The Justices Write Separately: Uses of the

Concurrence by the Rehnquist Court." *University of California-Davis Law Review* 23: 777–831.

Rehnquist, William H. 1987. *The Supreme Court*. New York: William Morrow.

Reuben, Richard D. 1991. "Scalia Is Still Taking Shots at O'Connor." *Los Angeles Daily Journal* (21 May 1991): 7.

Riggs, Robert. 1983. "Justice O'Connor: First Term Appraisal." *Brigham Young University Law Review* 1983: 1–46.

Riker, William. 1986. *The Art of Political Manipulation*. New Haven, Conn.: Yale University Press.

Roberts, Dorothy E. 1991. "Sandra Day O'Connor, Conservative Discourse, and Reproductive Freedom." *Women's Rights Law Reporter* 13: 95–104.

Rohde, David. 1972. "Policy Goals and Opinion Coalitions in the Supreme Court." *Midwest Journal of Political Science* 16: 208–24.

Sapiro, Virginia. 1983. *The Political Integration of Women*. Champaign, Ill.: University of Illinois Press.

Savage, David G. 1990. "Sandra Day O'Connor." In *Eight Men and a Lady: Profiles of the Justices of the Supreme Court*, ed. J. Joseph, 208–40. Bethesda, Md.: National Press.

Scarrow, Howard A. 1994. "Vote Dilution, Political Party Dilution, and the Voting Rights Act." A paper presented to the Annual Meeting of the American Political Science Association, New York City, 1–4 September 1994.

Scheb, John M. III, and Lee W. Ailshie. 1985. "Justice Sandra Day O'Connor and the 'Freshman Effect.' " *Judicature* 69: 9–12.

Schubert, Glendon. 1967. "Ideologies and Attitudes, Academic and Judicial." *Journal of Politics* 29: 3–40.

Schwartz, Bernard. 1993. *A History of the Supreme Court*. New York: Oxford University Press.

Schwartz, Edward P. 1992. "Policy, Precedent, and Power: A Positive Theory of Supreme Court Decision Making." *Journal of Law, Economics, and Organization* 8: 219–52.

Schwartz, Herman, ed. 1987. *The Burger Years: Rights and Wrongs in the Supreme Court*. New York: Penguin Books.

Segal, Jeffrey, and Harold Spaeth. 1993. *The Supreme Court and the Attitudinal Model*. New York: Cambridge University Press.

Segal, Jeffrey, Lee Epstein, Charles Cameron, and Harold Spaeth. 1995. "Ideological Values and the Votes of U.S. Supreme Court Justices Revisited." *Journal of Politics* 57: 812–23.

Shea, Barbara. 1986. "Sandra Day O'Connor—Woman, Lawyer, Justice: Her First Four Terms on the Court." *University of Missouri-Kansas City Law Review* 55: 1–32.

Sherry, Susana. 1986. "Civic Virtue and the Feminine Voice in Constitutional Adjudication." *Virginia Law Review* 72: 543–616.

Simon, James F. 1995. *The Center Holds*. New York: Simon and Schuster.

Slocum, Alfred. 1991. "At the Crossroads of Civil Rights: Tensions between the Wartime Amendments in the Jurisprudence of Justice O'Connor." *Women's Rights Law Reporter* 13: 105–12.

Smith, Rogers. 1988. "Political Jurisprudence, the 'New Institutionalism,' and the Future of Public Law." *American Political Science Review* 82: 89–108.

Songer, Donald, Sue Davis, and Susan Haire. 1994. "A Reappraisal of Diversification in the Federal Courts: Gender Effects in the Courts of Appeals." *Journal of Politics* 56: 425–39.

Spaeth, Harold, and Michael Altfeld. 1985a. "Influence Relationships within the Supreme Court: A Comparison of the Warren and Burger Courts." *Western Political Quarterly* 38: 70–83.

——— 1985b. "Measuring Power on the Supreme Court: An Alternative to the Power Index." *Jurimetrics Journal* 26: 48–75.

Spiller, Pablo. 1992. "Rationality, Decision Rules, and Collegial Courts." *International Review of Law and Economics* 12: 186–90.

Steamer, Robert. 1986. *Chief Justice*. Columbia, S.C.: University of South Carolina Press.

Strauss, David A. 1992. "Abortion, Toleration, and Moral Uncertainty." *Supreme Court Review* 1992: 1–28.

Sullivan, Kathleen. 1992a. "Post-Liberal Judging: The Roles of Categorization and Balancing." *University of Colorado Law Review* 63: 928.

——— 1992b. "The Justices of Rules and Standards." *Harvard Law Review* 106: 24–123.

——— 1993. "Categorization, Balancing, and Governmental Interests." In *Public Values in Constitutional Law*, ed. S. Gottlieb, 241–66. Ann Arbor, Mich.: University of Michigan Press.

Swanson, Wayne R. 1990. *The Christ Child Goes to Court*. Philadelphia, Pa.: Temple University Press.

"Symposium: Justice Sandra Day O'Connor." 1991. *Women's Rights Law Reporter* 13: 143–47.

"Symposium: the Voting Rights Act After *Shaw v. Reno*." 1995. *PS: Political Science and Politics* 28: 24–56.

Tate, C. Neal. 1981. "Personal Attribute Models of Voting Behavior of U.S. Supreme Court Justices: Liberalism in Civil Liberties and Economic Decisions." *American Political Science Review* 75: 355–67.

Taylor, Stuart. 1989. "Swing Vote on the Constitution." *American Lawyer* 11: 66–71.

Tong, Rosemary. 1989. *Feminist Thought: A Comprehensive Introduction*. Boulder, Colo.: Westview.

Toobin, Jeffrey. 1993. "The Burden of Clarence Thomas." *The New Yorker* (27 September 1993): 38–51.

——— 1995. "Chicken Supreme." *The New Yorker* (14 August 1995): 81–82.

Ulmer, S. Sidney. 1971. *Courts as Small and Not So Small Groups*. New York: General Learning.

VanGeel, T.R. 1991. *Understanding Supreme Court Opinions*. New York: Longman.

Walker, Thomas, Lee Epstein, and William Dixon. 1988. "On the Mysterious Demise of Consensual Norms in the U.S. Supreme Court." *Journal of Politics* 50: 361–89.

Weiser, Benjamin, and Joan Biskupic. 1993. "The Marshall Files: Secrets of the High Court." *The Washington Post* (23 May 1993): A1.

Wenzel, James. P. 1994. "Modeling Value Conflict on the U.S. Supreme Court." A paper presented to the Annual Meeting of the Midwest Political Science Association, Chicago, 14–18 April 1994.

Wermiel, Stephen J. 1991. "O'Connor—A Dual Role: An Introduction." *Women's Rights Law Reporter* 13: 129–42.

Winkle, John W. III, and Kevin Axelrod. 1992. "Subgroup Stability in the Rehnquist Court." A paper presented to the annual meeting of the Midwest Political Science Association, Chicago, 12–15 April 1992.

Witt, Elder. 1986. *A Different Justice: Reagan and the Supreme Court*. Washington, D.C.: Congressional Quarterly Press.

Wohl, Alexander. 1989. "O'Connor, J., Concurring." *ABA Journal* 75: 42–48.

Index

abortion rights, 6, 17, 25, 28, 33, 44, 56, 69, 91–92, 100–101, 104, 105n7, 110, 134; and privacy rights (*see also Roe v. Wade*), 17–18, 93; trimester approach, 31–32, 63, 93, 95, 97, 102; "unduly burdens" test, 32–34, 46n5, 46n8, 62–63, 94–98, 100, 101–2, 104; and viability, 31, 32, 62, 93–95, 98, 102–3

affirmative action, 6, 17, 28, 36, 64–65, 107–10, 116, 121, 121n1, 122n3, 122n4, 122n7; minority set-asides 23n3, 115–16; remedial purpose of 65, 108–9, 110–11, 114–17, 121; and reverse discrimination, 110–11, 113

Akron v. Akron Center for Reproductive Health, 32, 46n5, 94, 97, 103

anti-bright-line jurisprudence, 20–21, 26, 31–32, 33, 37, 38, 40, 41, 43, 44, 56, 69, 85, 95–97, 109, 119, 120, 123n8, 130, 132

balancing approaches, use of, 3, 8n4, 16, 20–21, 22, 29, 31, 33, 39–44, 56, 67, 69, 76, 95, 102, 132

Bandemer v. Davis, 70n2, 111–13

behavioral accommodationism (*see also* majority-side membership; O'Connor, Sandra Day, concurring behavior), 3–4, 5–6, 26, 30, 56, 68,

79, 84, 94, 98, 103, 109, 110, 120, 128

Bowen v. Roy, 83–85

Burger Court, ix, 2, 7, 29, 41, 44, 49–50, 63, 70n4, 71n7, 76, 123n9, 124n15, 127, 134; conservatism of 2, 27–28, 51, 81, 123–24n9; polarization of 7, 28, 34, 44, 64, 69, 111, 131

capital punishment, 15, 40; and juveniles, 40–41

Capitol Square Review and Advisory Board v. Pinette, 130–131

centrist justices, role of, 4–5, 7, 41, 44, 69, 96, 134; on the Burger Court, 7, 28, 37, 50–51, 111; on the Rehnquist Court, 6, 40, 43, 56, 69, 82, 94, 100–103, 109, 128–31, 134, 135n4

City of Richmond v. J. A. Croson Co., 109–10, 114–17

Civil Rights Act, Title VII, 64

coalition formation, collegial court setting, 3–6, 26, 29, 31, 53, 62, 64, 101, 105n6, 128, 134; and consensual norms, 5–7, 38, 54–56, 61, 68, 133–34

concurring opinions (*see also* O'Connor, Sandra Day, concurring behavior), 4–5, 30, 53–56, 61, 64, 71n6, 86, 119, 124n16, 134; and signaling

149

About the Author

Nancy Maveety is associate professor of political science at Tulane University, where she has taught since 1986. She received her Master's and Ph.D. in political science from the Johns Hopkins University.

Her first book, *Representation Rights and the Burger Years* (Ann Arbor: University of Michigan Press, 1991), offered one of the first revisionist accounts of the Burger Court and emphasized that court's contribution to the law of political representation. Maveety has also authored several articles for political science journals and law reviews on topics in judicial process and constitutional law. She is an active participant in several political science associations.

Maveety resides in New Orleans with her partner Tom and her cat Eightball. All three are avid fans of Carnival and Jazz Fest.

,